The Log Home Maintenance Guide

A Field Guide for Identifying, Preventing, and Solving Problems

Gary Schroeder

D1597255

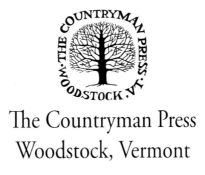

The Countryman Press
Woodstock, Vermont

Author
Gary Schroeder

Copy Editor
Kathy Schroeder

Design, Graphics, and Layout
Doug Todd

Acknowledgements
Special thanks goes out to the many people who have
helped make this publication possible:

James Adkins; Pat & Jean Allen; Lana & Clif Branum; Denise Carlson; Lilah Crowe;
Mike Howard; David Knox; Debbie Basset, Sashco; Don Bergstrom, Bergstrom Log Homes
& Restoration; Jerry & Carol Gray, Lone Pine Chinking; Wayne Konecki, Creative Carpentry;
Travis Ogilvie, Ogilvie Painting; Bob & Brenda Schnauffer, Schnauffer's Finishing Touch

The Staff of the Edmunds Company; The Staff of Schroeder Log Home Supply, Inc.;
The Forest History Center, Grand Rapids, MN; The Forest Products Laboratory, Madison, WI

© 2003 Log Home Guide Information Center, Inc.
P.O. Box 671, Grand Rapids, MN 55744-0671
www.lhgic.com   1-888-345-LOGS (5647)

First Edition

Library of Congress Cataloging-in-Publication Data
Log Home Guide Information Center, Inc.
    The log home maintenance guide : a field guide for indentifying, preventing, and
repairing problems / the Log Home Guide Information Center, Inc.,—1st ed.
        p. cm.
    Includes bibliographical references.
    ISBN 0-88150-585-4
    1. Log cabins—Maintenance and repair. I. Title.
TH4840.L645 2003
690'.837'0288—dc21   2003048593

Published by The Countryman Press, P.O. Box 748, Woodstock, Vermont 05091
Distributed by W. W. Norton & Company, Inc., 500 Fifth Avenue, New York, NY 10110

Printed in China

10 9 8 7 6 5 4 3 2 1

"We may use wood with intelligence only if we understand wood."

Frank Lloyd Wright, 1928

Contents

How to Use This Guide

My Log Home's History

This area is provided for you to keep pertinent information about your log home. A place is provided for a picture of your log home and for writing your own caption.

Chapter 1:
Care of Logs Before Building

For those of you who are in the planning stages of your log house, this section provides information about the care of logs and the importance of using a sapstain control.

Chapter 2:
Design for Easy Maintenance

This section explains maintenance-conscious design considerations that apply whether you are planning a new log home, contemplating an addition, or beginning a remodeling project. This section also reveals what may have caused problems for owners of existing log structures.

Chapter 3:
Log Inspection

A look at the factors involved as you inspect your house for maintenance problems concerning air and water infiltration, signs of rot, settling issues, and more.

Chapter 4: Insects

A look at the main problem-causing insects that affect log homes, with practical methods for preventing infestations as well as dealing with them.

Chapter 5:
Log Home Pests

This section looks at non-insect pests that frequently affect log homes, what you can do to protect your home against them, and how to fix the damage they cause.

Chapter 6:
Caulking & Chinking

Step-by-step information on installing backer rod and chinking, caulking a log home, and how to repair caulk and chinking problems.

Chapter 7:
Log Home Finishes

Practical information about log home stains and finishes, considerations when purchasing a finish, and how to figure the amount of finish needed for your project, as well as troubleshooting of stain and finish problems for your home.

Chapter 8: Log Home Decks

An overview of finishing decks, old and new, followed by troubleshooting of deck finish problems.

Chapter 9: Log Restoration

This section allows you to see log crown, half-log, and full-log replacement work being done in the field. Information on borate wood preservatives, impel rods, and wood epoxies is also included.

Chapter 10:
Cedar Shake & Shingle Roofs

For those of you with shake roofs, this section has you covered.

Introduction

A common misconception of log homebuyers is that log homes are impervious to the elements and are built to last forever with little maintenance. They point to the great Scandinavian log structures of Europe, which have stood for centuries as marvels of log and timber construction.

The truth of the matter is that many of those log structures have succumbed to the elements, mostly by fire. The ones still left standing have been either moved to open air museums or have been designated as such.

The secret of their longevity is due to a number of factors, the first being the use of old growth pine. This ancient, slow-growing pine was mostly heartwood and was extremely durable and resilient to fungus and insect infestation. The pine that is used today in construction is fast-grown, fourth and fifth generation trees and is comprised mostly of sapwood, which is many times more insect and fungus prone.

Great care was also given to the selection and felling of the logs. Choice pine trees had their branches and tops cut off and were left to stand for years before finally being cut down. This process was called "girdling" and allowed the pine's natural resins to bleed upwards and out through the severed tree branches, making the entire tree resinous and far more rot resistant than a tree that had been cut and dried. This fully cured, rot-resistant pine tree was called an ore-pine by ancient Europeans.

Today, old-growth pine is difficult, if not impossible, to obtain; and few if any loggers would be willing to girdle and allow the trees to stand for years before felling them.

Like the pines, cedar used for both decking and shake roofs contains little hardwood and is not as rot- and insect-resistant as its ancestors. Thujaplicins are naturally occurring chemicals found in the heartwood of cedar that are responsible for that species' rot resistance and insect resistance. The less heartwood, the less rot resistance.

For a modern day log structure to withstand the elements and endure the test of time, the structure needs to successfully meet four critical criteria:

1. The structure must be of quality construction.

2. The architectural design and landscaping of the structure must minimize the contact of logs with moisture.

3. The structure needs to be protected by a quality, water repellent finish, including the use of borate wood preservatives applied prior to finishing.

4. An established maintenance schedule for the exterior logs must be set up and followed.

My Log Home's History

The size of my home is: _____ feet wide by _____ feet long
Height of sidewalls is:_____ Roof pitch is: ___/12
Number of log courses is:_____ The length of the roof overhang is:_____ feet
Roof style: ❑ Gable ❑ Gambrel ❑ A-Frame ❑ Other:_____

My home is: ❑ Handcrafted ❑ Pre-cut ❑ Log Sided ❑ Cedar Sided
Other:_____

The year my house was built:_____
Wood species of log used:_____
The builder/manufacturer name is:_____

Stain or Finish Previously Used
Exterior:_____Deck:_____
Interior:_____
Brand/type of caulk or chinking used:_____Year_____
Brand/type of stain or finish used:_____Year_____

Place for My Log Home's Picture

FYI: The Parts of a Log

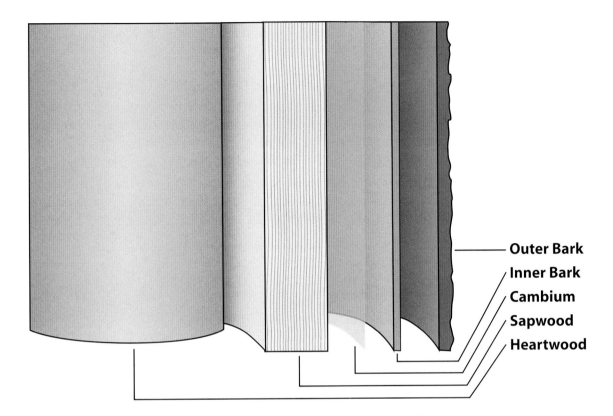

Outer Bark
Inner Bark
Cambium
Sapwood
Heartwood

Outer Bark The exterior protective layer that insulates the living tree from temperature extremes, rain, and many insect species. The outer bark consists of dead cells, unlike the inner bark.

Inner Bark Also known as the "Phloem," it is necessary to transfer food from the leaves throughout the rest of the living tree.

Cambium A very thin membrane layer of living cells responsible for producing new bark on one side and new sapwood on the other side. The cambium layer is usually only one cell thick and can act like a mill glaze if not removed during drawknifing. (Mill glaze is the stain-repelling film left over from shaping logs in the processing mill.)

Sapwood Also known as the "Xylem," this makes up the majority of most logs and is responsible for transferring water from the roots to the leaves. Fourth and fifth generation growth trees will consist mostly of sapwood.

Heartwood This is the central supporting structure of a mature tree. Heartwood consists of hard, aged, dead sapwood that in time fills with resins and waste material from the living sapwood. The heartwood of a tree is often distinctively darker and has smaller, tighter rings then sapwood. The older the tree, the more heartwood it will have. It is the heartwood of trees that contains the natural wood preservatives.

Chapter 1: Care of Logs Before Building

If you are building from logs that you have obtained, consider how you will be treating the logs and preparing them BEFORE construction begins.

"Checks"

Checks are cracks that open in the log as moisture evaporates from wet or "green" logs. Green wood is considered to contain a moisture content of 20 percent or more. Checks allow water and insects to infiltrate and cause future maintenance problems.

Minimize Checks in Dry Climates

To minimize the size and number of checks that can occur, cut either a 1 inch or 2 inch wide strip in the bark to the wood surface down the full length of the log on two opposing sides. Stack the logs in a pile at least two feet from the ground in either a crisscross style or with dry wood spacers between the logs. Leave space between logs to allow air circulation. Keep the area under the logs free of grass, weeds, or anything that could prevent air circulation and hold moisture. Cover the logs loosely with a tarp to protect them from the sun and rain. Provide open space at the sides and ends of the tarp to allow air to circulate freely in and around the logs.

Minimize Checks in Wet Climates

Once the trees have been cut, drawknife the logs to remove all of the bark as soon as possible. Use a sapstain control to protect peeled logs from mold and stain-causing fungi during the curing or "seasoning" stage. Mold, mildew, and sapstain increase the wood's ability to hold water, increasing the chances of decay as well as insect infestation. There are fungicidal products in the log home industry made specifically to provide a sapstain control, such as LogKeeper, Timber-TEC, TM-5 FT, and M-Guard, to name just a few.

Why Use Sapstain Control?

As logs are peeled or sawn, their surfaces are susceptible to sapstain fungi.

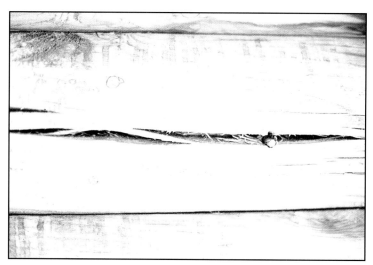

"Checks" are cracks that open in the log as moisture evaporates from wet or "green" logs.

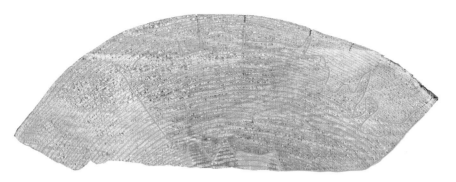

This digitally-enhanced cross section shows sapstain inside the wood. A sapstain control product was used to stop the sapstain from reaching the outer surface.

Fungi are tiny, threadlike organisms which utilize wood, or carbohydrates stored in wood cells, for food. Besides food, fungi require the presence of air (oxygen), water, and warm temperatures to survive and grow. These fungi, as they move through the wood, can leave behind a colored stain of blue, gray, black, red, or brown. It is most commonly known as **blue stain**. These are permanent discolorations and can be either an asset or a detriment, depending on your expectations of how the logs should look.

Sapstain does not affect the wood's strength, but it is important to note that it is nature's first step in preparing the wood for future rot. Sapstain occurs *in* the wood, while mildew (black) or mold (white) grow *on* the surface of logs or timbers and aid in the absorption of water into the wood.

To help prevent fungi from entering wood, spray the wood within 24 hours of drawknifing with Log Keeper, TM-5 FT, or another sapstain control. Apply the sapstain control late in the day so there is less chance of evaporation before it has penetrated the log surface. Do not spray prior to rain, for the spray will be washed off or diluted. **Note:** Species like balsam fir, spruce, and cedar are not as susceptible to sapstain as are the pines. Aspen and high moisture woods may need higher concentrations of sapstain control, as well as more frequent applications.

Stack the logs in a pile at least two feet from the ground in a crisscross style or use dry spacers to keep the logs from resting on each other. Wet wood on wet wood will harbor areas for sapstain or insects to work. Leave space between logs to allow air circulation. Keep the

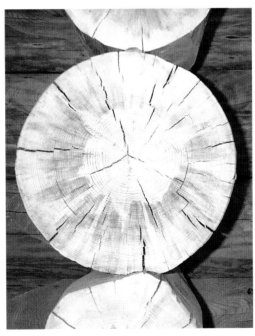

These logs were not treated with a sapstain control. The blue stain has a bluish-gray appearance.

Applying a sapstain control on new logs. Sapstain control products can be sprayed on, or the logs may be dip treated.

A tip for spraying: Mark the ends of the logs with an upward pointing arrow. Spray the logs thoroughly; when the logs have dried, turn the logs over and finish spraying them. The arrow will take any guesswork out of which side was coated and which side was not.

area under the logs free of grass, weeds, or anything that could prevent air circulation and hold moisture. Cover the logs loosely with a tarp to protect from the sun and rain. Provide open space at the sides and ends of the tarp to allow air to circulate freely in and around the logs.

Treat the Logs with Borates

Borate wood preservatives such as PeneTreat or Timbor are an effective way to protect logs and other woodwork from fungus and insect damage. The preservative is water-based and must be able to soak into bare wood, so it should be applied as soon as the logs have been debarked and before a sapstain control has been applied. See page 138 for more about borate wood preservatives.

Don't Build with the Bark Still On

Insects love to nest in the area between the bark and the wood; bark also absorbs moisture and seals moisture inside the log. Logs can be peeled with a drawknife, spud, or mechanical peeler.

Remove the Cambium and Inner Bark

The cambium layer is a thin, soft wood layer found between the sapwood and the inner bark of the log. This layer should be removed with a drawknife.

Some people like the look of peeled logs with some of the inner bark remaining. It gives the logs a rustic, striated, dark and light appearance. The problem with leaving the inner bark and underlying cambium on the logs is that finishes applied to the logs will adhere differently to the inner bark and sapwood, causing the finish to have premature adhesion failures. Also, the inner bark layer will darken over time, drastically changing the appearance of the logs. See page 103 for more about cambium on logs.

Ask Some Questions

If your log house will be built by a log crafter or purchased as a "kit" home, ask the builder or manufacturer what steps they take to prevent sapstain. Also ask if the logs will be spray-coated, dip treated, or pressure treated. Dip treatment is better than a spray coating, but pressure treatment is considered the best. Other questions should address what they do for protection against insects, and what steps they take to deal with settling issues.

Chapter 2: Design for Easy Maintenance

Wood + Heat + H$_2$O + Air = DECAY

Design is linked closely to maintenance. Wood decay and insect damage are the two main issues involving log homes. In order to prevent decay, we need to remove one of the ingredients for decay: Food (Wood), Heat, Water, or Air. The easiest one to control is Water. Rule Number 1 is to keep moisture—rain, runoff, back splashing—away from the logs of your house. Many wood damaging insects are attracted to moist and rotting wood. By minimizing moisture problems, you can effectively decrease the chance of insect and fungal infestation.

The sun can also do considerable harm through its damaging ultraviolet radiation. The sunniest sides of a house will always be the hardest hit by UV damage and will need to be monitored more closely than the other sides.

Provide Foundation Drainage

Allow water to run off as far away from your house as possible. The foundation grade should always slope away from the house (6 inches or more per 10 feet). Consider installing drain tile around the foundation to maximize drainage and prevent future problems.

Sill Logs Should Be 2 Feet Above Ground

Logs within the first 2 feet above ground level are more prone to decay than those higher up due to ground moisture and backsplashing problems.

Piled, melting snow and wet, decaying leaves pushed up along low sill logs can accelerate rot and decay. Ground soil should never come in contact with the logs for any extended length of time. For those of you in termite regions, an additional benefit of the 2-foot height

Sill logs should be a minimum of 2 feet above the ground.

This example shows what can happen when the endgrain of a log post is not protected from ground moisture.

A closeup view of algae growth and water blisters beneath the finish.

minimum for the sill logs is that the higher distance from the ground helps to act as a barrier against termite infestation.

Protect Log Posts from the Ground Up

Log posts need to be protected from ground moisture. The example shown above illustrates what can happen when the endgrain is not protected. Rainwater collected on the concrete slab and then migrated up into the unsealed endgrain of the post. The moisture collected between the wood surface and the finish coating, forming water blisters, and then algae began to grow. The dark streaks in the wood show where the log is starting to rot. This situation could have been avoided by sealing the endgrain of the log post with an end coating. Read more about log posts on pages 130–133.

Keep Exterior Walls Free of Backsplashing Hazards

In the photograph below, the lower logs have rotted due to rainwater backsplashing from the deck and onto the painted logs. A longer roof overhang would have prevented this costly log replacement. Paint is not recommended for logwork because it is a nonbreathable finish. See pages 160–162 for more information about painted logs. Lawn sprinklers, sidewalks, or obstacles such as stacks of firewood, propane or fuel oil tanks that have been placed near the drip line, or anything that redirects water toward the house instead of away from it, needs to be either removed or properly sheltered. Foundation vegetation can inhibit airflow around the bottom logs, creating a humid environment that will promote wood rot.

Include a "Maintenance Perspective"

As you review house plans and layouts, consider how the house design will be affected by the elements of sun, wind, and rain. Remember, dry wood does not rot. Avoid timesaving or cost-cutting decisions that will lead to future problems. Always consider how design and construction decisions will be impacted by moisture or rain, whether light mists or wind-driven downpours. Also consider the impact that insects may have.

The lower logs have rotted due to rainwater backsplashing from the deck onto the painted logs. Replacement logs have just been installed. A longer roof overhang would have prevented this costly log repair.

An example of self-draining, hand-scribed notches. See how the notch cuts are "tipped" and angled so that water will drain down and away from the notch, as opposed to draining back into the corner notches and lateral grooves.

This dovetail-style log structure has stood the test of time with a notch that has self-draining properties. Notice how the notches are cut at angles to let water drip down the length of the corner, as opposed to collecting and sitting on top of the logs.

Use a Self-Draining Notch Style

A self-draining notch is a necessary design element to minimize the amount of maintenance work needed during the life of the structure. The Log Building Standards that were developed by the International Log Builders' Association require hand-scribed log homes to have self-draining notches.

"Butt and pass" log corners often have this problem. The photo on the right shows how rainwater, snow, and ice can build up and puddle on the top of the log, eventually breaking down the finish. Water will begin working its way into the wood fiber, joinery, and eventually into the interior of the house. Caulking, chinking, and log home finishes are neither designed nor intended to protect against standing water. Dovetail-styled logs and hand-crafted full logs are two of the best log styles for self-draining notches due to curved surfaces and angled notch cuts.

Rainwater, snow, and ice can build up and puddle on the top of the log, eventually breaking down the finish. Water will begin working its way into the wood fiber, joinery, and eventually into the interior of the house.

Provide Adequate Venting

High moisture areas like kitchens and bathrooms need to be properly ventilated. Warm, moist air will collect and condense on ceiling logs and second story log floor joists, providing an environment for rot and decay to set in. If this problem is not detected early enough, serious structural damage can occur; some of the worst-case scenarios involve complete roof, wall, and floor joist replacement. Moisture content of 20 percent or higher of stained or finished logs should be cause for concern. A moisture meter is a valuable and handy tool for quickly monitoring the moisture content of your logs.

A digital moisture meter.

Log Ends Should Not Extend beyond Roof Eaves

Exposure of the log ends to the sun and rain can cause considerable damage. Protruding ends are highly susceptible to weathering and finish breakdown. Exposed endgrain acts like a sponge that can siphon rainwater deep within the log, causing future rot, decay, and insect infestation as well as structural weakness and possible roof damage.

Restoration costs for repairing this type of log damage can be staggering. If the roof is designed to have logs extended, cover the logs with either copper or a rubber roofing membrane.

Provide at Least a 2-Foot Roof Overhang

The longer, the better. Long overhangs provide increased protection from rain, snow, and the sun's damaging UV rays. The lack of substantial overhangs on log

houses is the result of attempting to cut costs; unfortunately the long term restoration and log replacement costs will far exceed any money that was saved in the short term.

Don't Use Paint or a Heavy Surface Coating On Your Logs

Paint is not recommended for log homes because it builds up a thick coating that does not allow the wood to "breathe." Moisture trapped behind a thick, heavy paint coating will cause the logs to rot from the inside out. Paint will also become brittle and will crack with age, allowing water to seep into the exposed wood and again, causing rot from the inside out.

A heavy surface coating.

Use a Quality Finish

There are many high quality finishes on the market that are designed and formulated for log homes. Be aware that clear finishes provide little or no UV protection, break down faster, and need to be reapplied more often than pigmented finishes. See *About Log Home Finishes* starting on page 84 for more information.

Dormer without flashing.

Lower logs with water damage.

Logs cleaned and refinished with a typical silver-colored flashing installed. Copper flashing is aesthetically more suited to blend in with the warm wood tones of log homes.

Use Rain Gutters and Downspouts

These are some of the most important pieces of preventative maintenance hardware you can install on your log home.

Use Flashing on Dormers

Dormers are susceptible to weathering and wood rot. A common mistake is to not install flashing around the bottom edge of the dormer walls. In time, the lower logs will darken from water damage and fungal growth caused by backsplashing from roof runoff and melting snow.

A 3-inch to 4-inch metal flashing will prevent water damage to the lower logs. Copper flashing, though more expensive, is aesthetically more suited for blending in with the warm wood tone finishes of log homes. The flashing should be installed as part of the roof construction. When large logs are used, a flashing curb or lift can be used to provide extra space between the lower logs and the shingles. Flashing can be installed afterwards, as in the case of this house, but considerably more work and expense are involved.

Use Impel Rods

As a preventative maintenance step, impel rods can be installed in the two bottom courses of logs and near window and door jambs as the house is being constructed. Impel rods are concentrated rods of boron that are activated by moisture to protect the logs from rot and insect infestation. See pages 138–139 for additional information about impel rods and borate wood preservatives.

Cover Decks to Minimize Backsplashing and UV Damage

A covered porch provides more protection than an uncovered deck. Large expanses of unsheltered decking will always be a high maintenance area of your home. A 6-foot overhang shelters the 12-foot deck on this house. Though not a complete covering of the deck, the overhang helps to minimize rainstorm backsplashing and UV damage.

Use a Roof Membrane and Water Shield between Decking and Joist Logs
Unsheltered decks built on extended house log joists can suffer serious structural damage due to rot.

The Problem What typically happens is that the decking boards are nailed or screwed into unprotected, flattened-off portions of the logs; rainwater soaks the logs, collecting beneath the bottom of the decking and the top of the flat-

tened log. It is this area that will begin to rot. Checks and cracks will open in the top of the log allowing more water to seep in, and accelerating the decaying process. In time, the rot can spread inside the house, causing considerable structural damage and costly repairs.

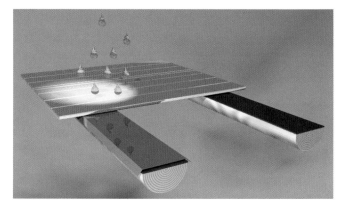

Flashing with 1 inch to 2 inches of drip edge over an adhesive-backed roofing membrane. Log ends can be profiled to shed rain more effectively.

Profiled logs (sideview).

ing a proper seal against air and water infiltration.

The profile view to the left shows how the two pieces of flashing work together. The top piece is secured to the chimney, while the bottom piece is secured to the roof. As the house logs dry and settle, the roof flashing can slide down behind the chimney flashing. Wall logs typically will settle from shrinkage between 6 inches to 10 inches depending on the type and diameter of the logs. Seasoned logs in a handcrafted Swedish cope home will typically shrink ½ inch per foot of wall height.

A Better Approach Install an adhesive-backed roofing membrane over the top of the log. The membrane will provide water repellency to the top of the log while sealing around the nails or deck screws that are used to secure the deck-ing. Next, a metal flashing with an angled drip edge to shed water over the sides of the log is installed. Decking is then nailed or screwed down. The log ends can also be profiled to improve water runoff and minimize end rot. See *Log Restoration* starting on page 134.

Use Two-Piece Copper Flashing on Chimneys

Copper flashing lasts longer than aluminum or sheet metal flashing. The importance of a two-piece flashing for log structures is that it allows the roof structure to settle and "slide" down around the chimney while maintain-

Use two-piece copper flashing on chimneys. Copper flashing lasts longer than aluminum or sheet metal flashing.

Chapter 3: Log Inspection

Log homes and structures have been a mainstay of American architecture since the first colonists arrived in Virginia in the early 1600s. Though their early histories usually revolve around initial settlement, with the dwellings being abandoned after frame or masonry structures could be built, these originals can still be found throughout North America.

Over the past 60 years the popularity of these historic buildings, coupled with the increasing interest and construction of modern milled and hand-crafted log homes, has brought forth issues that few people think of when they were making the initial purchase of the building.

Being made almost entirely of exposed wood, log homes have a tendency to become very decrepit in appearance if left for long periods without maintenance. Dirty, faded logs are not necessarily a problem. Though UV radiation damages the surface cells of the logs, it is seldom the primary cause for structural damage. The causes of most homeowners' headaches are water damage, rot, and insect infestation. There are other repair and restoration issues, but these three things are the most common and lead to the costliest repairs and in worst-case scenarios, if left unattended, leave the house uninhabitable.

It sounds pretty bad, but in reality it takes a while for truly irreparable damage to happen. If the problems can be identified, they can usually be reversed, if caught soon enough.

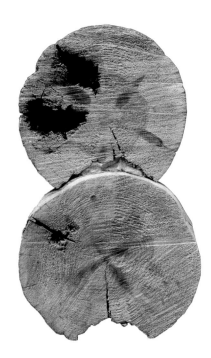

Log rot caused by water entering a crack in the log is shown in this cut-away view.

Where to Start

An inspection of the structure as well as the property is always a good place to begin. This will not only help identify situations that need to be addressed, but will also in many cases uncover the root cause that started the deterioration to begin with. Inspections should be done at least annually and usually in the spring so any repairs can be scheduled during the coming work season.

It is always a good idea to take notes when doing the inspection. This will give you something to compare to from inspection to inspection to see if there are changes.

Photographs are also an excellent way of keeping up with the aging of a structure from inspection to inspection. The more documentation you have to go on, the better chance there is of finding and arresting problems before they progress too far.

Also, when doing the inspection it's a good idea to have a pocketknife or scratch awl handy. Most deterioration will be visually evident, but sometimes it's necessary to poke and prod at the logs to check their integrity.

A good starting place for any home inspection is out in the yard around the house. This is especially true if you are in a forested area. Most of us enter our homes or properties from one direction, and really never pay close attention to the structure as we are approaching. Even though we spend time mowing the lawn and trimming the hedges, we don't pay attention to the building. Face it; we're doing something else, which at the time is more important.

When you do your annual or biannual inspection, step back from the house or outbuilding you are looking at, and see if anything stands out. You might be surprised at what you find. Some log deterioration happens so slowly that we just don't notice it until we really look.

Start from the Ground Up

Log home inspections are best done from the ground up. Most log deterioration starts with a water or moisture problem of some sort. Some problems can start with leaky gutters or poor water evacuation from the roof, and are higher up on the wall and in the soffits; but most start near the ground, and are a result of poor water drainage away from the building. Also, if you start

at the ground, you've usually found the end result of a problem higher up, because water will always seek the lowest point possible to migrate.

Signs to look for are dark areas on the bottom courses of logs and around the bottoms of windows. If you have a structure that is irregularly shaped (more than four walls), you also need to check the corners that intersect under the roof valleys. It is also important to examine the fascia boards (trim that gutters are attached to), and check for discoloration.

For those with wooded lots, pay particular attention to stumps and dead or fallen trees. Look for insect infestation. It's easy to identify. The tree or stump will usually be damp, there will be holes in the surface, and in most cases there will be piles of sawdust all around the base. This is a very natural occurrence, but it is not one that needs to happen in close proximity to your home.

If you find evidence of infestation, contact your local agricultural extension agent, or a licensed exterminator to get information on what can be done to remedy the situation. See *Chapter 4: Insects* starting on page 30 for more information about insects and their treatment.

Once you have investigated and noted items that need to be taken care of in the yard, and visually identified questionable areas on the structure's walls, it's time to check out the area around the foundation and first courses of log. The first thing to observe is the condition of the landscaping. It is important that proper air movement be allowed

Left & Above: Brown rot (also known as dry rot) decays the wood, turning it brown and leaving it soft, crumbly, and powdery. This causes serious structural damage and typically attacks the sill logs though it will affect trusses, rafters, and other structural wood components as well.

Mushrooms growing on logs are always a bad sign. The white patches of mildew are just as bad.

all the way around the house. A good rule of thumb is to make sure that there is at least 2 feet of open space between the landscaping and bottom courses of log.

If airflow is impeded, the sill and first courses of log have a tendency to stay damp. This is the point at which, if left untreated, two things are going to occur: rot or insect infestation—or both. There is not a log coating on the market that will hold up to continuously damp conditions. Once the coating fails, spores from all sorts of rot-causing fungis can get at the raw damp wood, which serves as an excellent food source.

If the logs are damp and discolored, probe the area with your pocketknife or scratch awl to see if the wood is soft or "punky" (extremely soft and flaky). Also examine any fissures or checks in the logs to see if they show any telltale signs of fruiting bodies (fungus) or shaving piles (insect infestation). If insects are present, there will also

Algae (blue-green) will attack wood if the moisture percentage is greater than 19 percent.

An example of a sill log that was placed too close to the ground. Deterioration of the wood was caused by a combination of brown rot and algae.

be small piles of sawdust on the top curvatures of the logs and around the foundation.

Pay particular attention to the junction between log walls and outdoor decks. Read more about decks in Chapter 8 (pages 120–133). If a ledger board (2x stock nailed parallel and directly to the log) has been used, make certain no water-absorbing debris has accumulated between the deck boards. This is a primary area to find places where water can stand, and if left unattended a good place to find a rotted log.

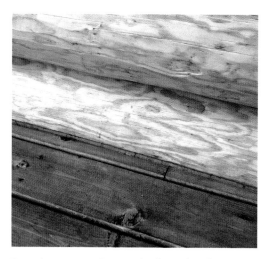

Pay close attention to the junction between log walls and decks.

This is also a good time to check the foundation itself. Cracks in the rockwork or brick show that the foundation has settled. This is not necessarily a bad thing. All foundations settle to some extent. Note the occurrence and check to see if the fissure increases in size over the next few inspections. One thing that does need to be examined is the fissures themselves. If large enough, they can be used as travel thoroughfares for carpenter and other ant species as well as termites.

You can check for termite infestation by looking at the interior of the masonry from inside the crawlspace. If termites are or have been present, there will be mud tunnels leading from the ground to the sill log or sub-floor band. If these tunnels are present, call an exterminator immediately for proper advice on how to handle the situation. Read more about termites on pages 39–40.

If it doesn't seem that improper air movement is the cause of the damp conditions around the bottom courses of logs, explore farther up the wall. Check under and around door and window casings. If the tops of the door and window casings have not been properly flashed and the sides sufficiently sealed with caulking, wind-driven rain or runoff from higher up

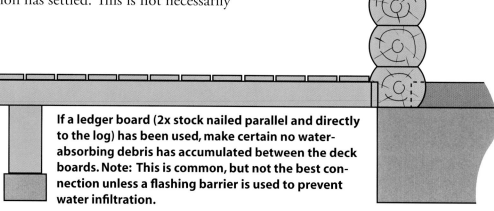

If a ledger board (2x stock nailed parallel and directly to the log) has been used, make certain no water-absorbing debris has accumulated between the deck boards. Note: This is common, but not the best connection unless a flashing barrier is used to prevent water infiltration.

The decimated remains of a termite-infested stump.

minor adjustments, while others can be of a much more serious nature involving major reconstruction performed by professional log restoration contractors.

It is also a good time to examine the corner notching. In log buildings, the corners are a primary structural entity in the building. Unfortunately, they are also an excellent place for fungus to grow. Because of the large amount of exposed end grain, and the many vertical cuts in the notches, water can easily infiltrate the logs in this area.

A spiked log home with settling problems. The opened joints allow water and insects to easily enter the home.

will seep behind them. This will cause a moisture problem in the exposed end grain of the logs around the door and window openings. In the case of windows, excessive amounts of water will seep out the bottom and continue down the wall.

Also check the condition of the screw jacks and make any adjustments necessary. In some cases, the builder will do the routine adjustments to the screw jacks as the house settles, or will give specific instructions to the owner on when and how to make adjustments to the jacks.

If your home appears to be experiencing settling problems, consult with the builder or manufacturer. Some settling problems are easily solved with only

If the notches have not been caulked, now might be a good time to look into getting it done. This is also true of the joints between the logs themselves. If they have been caulked or chinked,

An example of poor craftsmanship and a lack of regular maintenance. Chink joints should not be wider than the logs. Insects have littered the lower logs with tunnels and decay has set into the unfinished logs, making the structural integrity of this house questionable. The long uncovered log ends have acted like straws to suck moisture into the logwork.

examine them to see if any cracking in the material has occurred. This sometimes happens because of excessive shrinkage of the logs.

There are a number of excellent hand-crafters out there that cut their homes so tight that it is felt that no caulking is needed. The caulk and chinking products are fairly cheap, as opposed to any repair bills that come in later because some anomalous factor caused the joint to open and accept water, which in turn caused rot.

When examining the walls, also pay attention to the stain coating, if there is one. The sun's UV radiation is the key predator of stain coatings and the surface wood below them. If the stain is faded or has eroded, yet the wood is dry, it is probably time to think about restaining.

The amount of stain wear that shows from one log course to the next on the building will vary with the amount of direct wind and weather that the walls receive. Walls that stay mostly shaded, assuming no serious water problems are detected, will probably show more signs of mildew growth after the stain has run its effective life. Mildew is not necessarily harmful to the wood, but it is fairly unsightly.

After you have checked the sills and the windows, the corners and the joints, if you still haven't identified the source of the water problem, check the soffits, fascias, and the flashed area where the chimney and roof meet. Often, stopped up gutters or gutters that have pulled away from the fascia will cause water to wick back under the shingles and down the fascia across the soffit, and down the wall.

At valley rafter terminuses (at the top of the wall) pay particular attention to the log intersections below. This is especially key where stopped up gutters are involved. Gutters should be checked and cleaned a minimum of once a year in the late fall. In some regions, including the Southeast and Mid-Atlantic, this should also be done in the spring.

If it is found that water is seeping down the chimney and leaking back onto the logs, check the flashing to ensure that it hasn't been damaged. If it has, or if no flashing is present, contact a roofing contractor to see what can be done. Remember that coal tar (roofing tar) is not a proper material to use as a primary flashing material.

At this point the sources of your problems have been identified. Remember that there is a solution for every problem. Some solutions are more costly than others, but nothing is as costly as ignoring the problem. With a proper annual or semi-annual inspection these situations can be put in check, and you can spend more time enjoying the structure, instead of worrying about when it's going to fall down around you.

Vertical log structures, like the log post on page 14, must be sealed and protected to keep moisture from wicking upward into the log and attracting decay and insects. See pages 131–132 for more information.

Chapter 4: Insects

Name	About	Exit Holes	Damage	Treatment
Ambrosia Beetles, page 32	Family Platypodidae. 1/8 in. to 1/5 in. long and darkly colored. Only 6–10 weeks from egg to adult state. Attracted to newly felled green wood with 48% to 50% moisture content or higher.	Size varies depending on species. Galleries are darkly stained with sapstain fungus.	Bores directly into newly felled sapwood of conifers and inoculates a black sapstain fungus into the wood. Fungus will spread as galleries are enlarged. Some species will infest heartwood.	Remove felled trees immediately from the forest. Dip or spray treat newly felled logs in a borate preservative such as PeneTreat to prevent and eradicate infestation.
Bark Beetles, page 33	Family Scolytidae and Platypodidae. Includes the Ips beetle, or engraver beetle. They need both bark and sapwood in order to infest. 1/50 in. to 1/8 in. long.	1/16-in. diameter exit holes in bark of trees.	Damage occurs after felling of trees. Larvae chew galleries between bark and sapwood leaving an engraved look to the surface of the sapwood. Some species inoculate wood with wood decaying sapstain fungus. They do not reinfest.	Drawknife trees immediately. Treat logs with a borate wood preservative to kill off infestation. Discard affected logs or lumber during the building stage of house. They do not reinfest wood. Sapstain discoloration cannot be removed from wood.
Carpenter Ants, page 34	Large black ants up to 1/2 in. long. Over 500 species worldwide. Attracted to wet decaying wood for nesting.	Size varies depending on species.	They do not eat wood, just build extensive nesting galleries. Can cause structural damage to logs and timbers.	Locate and destroy nest. Spray holes with a carpenter ant insecticide, then seal holes with caulking. Check and treat logs and woodwork for signs of excessive moisture and decay.
Carpenter Bees, page 35	Large bees about 1 in. long. Abdomen is black and hairless. Attracted to dry wood. Males fiercely protect entrance holes by buzzing loudly, but they cannot sting.	Circular, 1/2 in.	They do not eat wood, just build extensive nesting galleries. Can cause structural damage to logs and timbers. Nests attract woodpeckers that can cause more damage to wood.	Spray an insecticide for bees and wasps or carpenter ants into holes at night while they sleep. Cover holes with caulking. Reapply until they no longer emerge.
Flat-Headed Wood Borers, page 36	Family Buprestid. 1/4 in. to 1 1/4 in. Adults are metallic copper, green, blue, or black; larvae are flat-headed. Approximately 700 species in North America. Do not reinfest wood. Females lay eggs in freshly cut trees.	Oval and elongated. Size varies depending on species.	Larvae feed on the sapwood of both softwoods and hardwoods. Larvae can feed for 1 to 5 years, causing structural damage to logs and timbers.	Logs should be treated with a borate preservative to prevent and eradicate infestation before house is built. If they are emerging from house logs, spray an insecticide into holes and seal with caulking. Retreat as needed.

Name	About	Exit Holes	Damage	Treatment
Powderpost Beetles (Anobiids), page 37	Family Anobiidae. Reddish to dark brown and 1/16 in. to 3/8 in. long. Known as deathwatch beetles and furniture beetles. Attracted to wood over 20% moisture content. Emit powdery flour-like wood dust from tunnel entrances.	Circular, 1/16-in. to 1/8-in. diameter.	Will attack both soft and hardwoods. Can cause structural damage to logs and timbers.	Spray an insecticide into holes and seal with caulking. Retreat as needed.
Powderpost Beetles (Lyctids), page 37	Family Lyctidae. Reddish-brown to black and 1/8 in. to 5/16 in. long. Emit powdery flour-like wood dust from tunnel entrances.	Circular, 1/32 in. to 1/16 in. diameter.	Attacks seasoned or partially seasoned sapwood of hardwoods. Can cause structural damage with many tunnel galleries.	Spray an insecticide into holes and seal with caulking. Retreat as needed.
Round-Headed Wood Borers, page 38	Family Cerambycidae. Known as longhorned beetles and pine sawyers. Includes the old house borer. 1/4 in. to 3 in. long with very long antennae that can be three times the length of the body. Over 1200 species in North America. Larvae have round heads. Larval period can last from 2 to 3 years and as long as 15 years, depending on the moisture content of the wood.	Round to slightly oval; size varies depending on species. Old house borer tunnels are marked with tiny ringlets.	Can chew and tunnel through plasterboard, hardwood flooring, plywood and shingles. Prefers sapwood of coniferous trees. Can cause structural damage with many tunnel galleries.	Spray an insecticide into holes and seal with caulking. Retreat as needed.
Termites, page 39	Order Isoptera. 41 species in North America. 5 major groups of termites in the U.S.: subterranean, drywood, dampwood, powderpost, and Formosan. The subterranean is found throughout the U.S.	Small tube-shaped tunnels leading from the ground to the wooden structure; irregularly-shaped tunnel galleries in wood.	Attracted to both dry or damp wood depending on species. Can cause severe, house-condemning structural damage with many tunnel galleries.	Seek professional help from a termite exterminator.
Winter Flies, page 40	Cluster flies that are dark gray and larger than a housefly.	None	Does not cause damage, just annoyance.	Flyswatter, insect strips, or vacuum cleaner to control populations.
Wood Wasps, page 41	Also known as horntails. More than 1 in. long. Larval stage can take 2 to 5 years to reach adult. They will not reinfest.	Circular, 1/4 in. to 1/2 in.	Attacks sapwood and heartwood. Damage is mostly cosmetic, though galleries 10 in. to 12 in. long are constructed. Larvae can chew through plasterboard and hardwood floors.	Spray an insecticide into holes and seal with caulking. Retreat as needed.

General Treatment of Insects

Spot treatment insecticides can be injected into holes with a glue syringe. As a preventative measure, the use of borates such as PeneTreat before coating the wood with a finish helps to make infestation more difficult. Stain and finish additives such as CPF-2D can also be used to apply an insecticidal barrier to the wood. CPF-2D should only be used with exterior finishes. Do not use CPF-2D for interior finish applications. The use of polyurethane based caulking will aid in deterring insects because they have a natural repulsion to polyurethane products.

However you choose to rid your logs of insects, consider spraying borates into the tunnels afterwards to help guard against wood-decaying fungi. Just mix up some PeneTreat or other borates in a spray bottle or pump sprayer and administer it into the holes. Also, be sure to seal off the tunnel entrances by pounding in wooden dowels, by using caulking or wood putty, or by mixing a product like WoodEpox or LiquidWood with sawdust. See pages 134–137 for more info.

Ambrosia Beetles

These beetles are members of the Platypodidae family and though grouped in with bark beetles, they do not need bark in order to attack trees. Their heads curl downwards and are hidden beneath a hood-like middle body section called the thorax. These beetles get their name from the black ambrosia fungus that they farm in galleries within the wood they infest. Ambrosia beetles do not eat wood; instead, they use wood to build galleries and plant and harvest the ambrosia sapstain fungus to nurture their young. The galleries are also used for nesting and hatching of young. Ambrosia beetles will infest both softwood and hardwood trees.

Telltale signs of an Asian ambrosia beetle infestation are white toothpick-like protrusions from tiny pinholes in the wood surface. The protrusions are a compacted mixture of powdery sawdust, tree sap, and frass or fecal matter. Other species of ambrosia beetles will leave small pinholes and powdery wood dust at the base of the tree or log.

Telltale signs of an Asian ambrosia beetle infestation: white toothpick-like protrusions from tiny pinholes in the wood surface.

Prevention

Newly felled trees should be removed from the forest as soon as possible to avoid infestation. Dip or spray treat newly felled trees with a sapstain control and/or borate wood preservative to promote eradication and prevent infestation.

Treatment

If they have attacked your log home, spot treat the holes by injecting an insecticide such as CPF-2D with a syringe and seal holes with caulking or wood putty. Reapply as needed. The dark stains from the ambrosia sapstain fungus cannot be removed. You can also inject a sapstain control like LogKeeper or TM-5 First Treat into the holes to kill off the sapstain fungi and keep it from spreading.

Bark Beetles

This is a group of small beetles (adults are less than ¼ inch long) from the Scolytidae family which lay their eggs in the bark of trees. The coloration of bark beetles ranges from dark red to brown to black. The western pine beetle, the Ips beetles, and the red turpentine beetles all attack pine trees. Bark beetles need bark as an integral part of the reproductive cycle. The eggs are laid in galleries between the bark and the sapwood of the tree. Once hatched, the larvae feed on the inner bark.

The Western Pine Beetle (shown) has two to four generations each year. The adults build egg galleries that wind maze-like inside the infected log. Once the larvae hatch, they migrate towards the bark of the tree and feed on the inner bark. Adults attack the midtrunk of trees and then spread up and down throughout the tree.

The Ips Beetles consist of 25 species that will have anywhere from two to five generations each year. Like the ambrosia beetle, Ips beetles inoculate the infested wood with sapstain fungi to feed their young. Instead of ambrosia fungi, however, the Ips utilize the blue sapstain fungi. The Ips beetles are also known as engraver beetles because their young chew meandering engravings in the wood surface between the bark and the sapwood. This "engraved" wood is prized by some log furniture builders for its decorative quality.

The Red Turpentine Beetles *(Dendroctonus valens)* are the largest and the most widely distributed bark beetles in North America. They attack pines and sometimes fir, larch, and spruce trees and have up to three generations per year. Adults attack trees from 2 to 8 feet from the ground level. Their nesting galleries are located between the inner bark and sapwood of the tree.

Prevention

Because bark beetles need bark in order to reproduce, most of the damage is done while the trees are still growing or after they have been cut. If you are building your own log home, check for signs of bark beetle activity on the trees before felling. Dip or spray treating newly felled logs with borate wood preservatives and a sapstain control will help to eradicate and prevent infestations. Removing the bark from the trees as soon as possible can also reduce infestations.

Treatment

As noted above, borate wood preservatives and a sapstain control can be used once the trees have been felled.

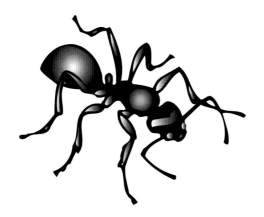

Carpenter Ants

Carpenter ants (*Camponotus herculeanus*) can sometimes be a problem if wood remains moist and wood rot occurs. Carpenter ants do not eat wood; instead they build nests in the decaying wood.

Prevention

Fix moisture problems that exist around the home, such as leaking roofs, cracks in the caulking, gaps in the log joints, rotting sill logs, clogged gutters or leaking plumbing.

Trim trees and shrubbery away from the house. Replace water-damaged or decayed wood. Wood should not be in contact with the soil. (This is also important in preventing termite damage. See page 39.)

Remove dead trees and stumps. A cleared area of 50 feet around the house is recommended. Remove or repair broken branches and any other damage to neighboring trees. Store firewood off of the ground and away from the house. This minimizes other problems with firewood insects.

Carpenter ant next to hole with fine, flour-like wood debris.

Carpenter ant shown among the squared logs of a dovetailed log home. The house had been sided over, giving the ants a safe refuge for nesting between the siding and the logs.

Winged carpenter ant entering a hole in the wood.

Treatment

Treat ant-infested areas with a borate wood preservative such as PeneTreat or an approved carpenter ant insecticide. Insecticidal sprays or boric acid dusts can be blown into tunnel entrances. If using dusts, avoid inhalation of dust. Also look for the cause of the moisture problems and eliminate them. Carpenter ants can enter a building by way of vegetation that may touch the building. To help prevent this, trim bushes and trees touching the building and watch for rotting stumps that could have underground root systems near your building. Finding and treating the brood location with a carpenter ant insecticide is the most direct method of treatment.

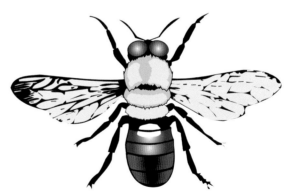

Carpenter Bees

The large carpenter bees (genus *Xylocopa*) are the ones that do the most damage to log homes, boring approximately ½-inch diameter tunnels into logs and other wood surfaces including decks, overhangs, and fence rails. The tunnels pose a threat of infestation of wood-decaying fungi or other insects, such as carpenter ants. The presence of carpenter bees can attract woodpeckers, which can do additional damage by widening existing holes and damaging nearby wood surfaces.

Carpenter bees, like carpenter ants, do not eat wood. They eat nectar from flowers and use wood for nesting purposes. Nesting galleries can be 10 inches to 12 inches in length with a number of nesting chambers extending out from the main gallery. Despite the damage they can do, carpenter bees are considered beneficial insects because of their assistance in pollination of various crops.

Prevention

Borate wood preservatives such as PeneTreat should be used before the logs are finished. Though this is not a foolproof method of preventing carpenter bee infestation, it will definitely act as a hindrance. Carpenter bees are attracted to dry, bare wood surfaces, so maintaining the finish of logs and trim can also help to prevent infestation. Early detection through periodic inspections of the trim and logwork will minimize damage.

Treatment

Insecticidal sprays and dusts are available to treat carpenter bees. These types of products may need to be applied every couple of weeks for a while to ensure effectiveness. Apply the insecticides at night while the hive is asleep and then seal entrance holes with caulking for maximum impact.

Be aware that some insecticides have been banned but not yet removed from store shelves. Consider the potential health risks of using such poisons around your home (young children are the most susceptible). If you have an exterminator do the job professionally, find out what they are using and if those chemicals have been banned in your area.

If you are having or have had problems with carpenter bees, consider adding CPF-2D or other contact insecticide to your finish when you recoat your house. If chemicals aren't your bag, you can give the kids a project with a couple of fly swatters. The males don't sting and the females are known to be more reluctant in stinging, unlike other bees, wasps, and hornets.

Flat-Headed Wood Borers

These beetles are from the family Buprestid and compose approximately 700 species in North America. The adults are metallic copper, green, blue, or black with some having brightly colored irregular spots marking their wings. Because of their metallic appearance, they are also known as metallic wood borers. The name "flat-headed" comes from the head shape of the beetles during the larval stage.

The flat-headed wood boring beetles are attracted to freshly cut softwoods for nesting. The female will lay eggs in small checks that develop as the wood begins to dry. Once the eggs hatch, the larvae bore farther into the sapwood for feeding. These borers feed deeper and deeper into the wood as it dries but they do not feed on heartwood. The larvae can feed inside the sapwood anywhere from one to five years (depending on the amount of moisture in the log) doing a significant amount of damage. These particular beetles will not reinfest logs nor are they attracted to dry wood.

Prevention

Borate wood preservatives such as PeneTreat should be used before the logs are finished—dip treating is considered the best method. Some sapstain control products have insecticidal properties and are helpful by killing the beetles before they emerge.

Treatment

If beetles begin to emerge from the logs you can try injecting insecticides like CPF-2D or boric acid powders into the holes to eradicate remaining insects before they emerge. Once the holes are treated, seal with caulking. Reapply as necessary until the beetles are no longer a problem.

Powderpost Beetles

Refers primarily to two groups of the Coleoptera order—lyctids and anobiids. The term "powderpost" comes from the powdery sawdust and fecal matter that is emitted from their tunnels.

The Anobiidae (pronounced an-no-bee-i-dee) are the smallest of the powderpost beetles, ranging from ¹⁄₁₆

inch to ⅜ inch long. They are reddish to dark brown and are attracted to wood with a moisture content over 19 percent. They are known to infest and reinfest both hardwoods and softwoods leaving numerous ⅛-inch circular holes. The larvae will tunnel throughout the wood for as long as two to three years before reaching adulthood and laying eggs, and then emerging.

The anobiids are also known as furniture beetles and deathwatch beetles. The term "deathwatch" comes from the Middle Ages. The beetle communicates by tapping its head on wood, and people in the Middle Ages who were staying up late with the sick and dying would hear their tappings.

Anobiids require a higher wood moisture content than the lyctids. Because of this, high-humidity coastal areas and unheated wooden structures or crawlspaces are quite attractive to them. Infested wood will become a maze of honeycomb galleries that can, in time, cause structural problems. Anobiids will also reinfest wood and lumber and so can be quite problematic to the homeowner.

The Lyctidae (pronounced lick-ted-dee) are larger than the anobiids, measuring from ⅛ inch to ⁵⁄₁₆ inch long. They primarily attack the sapwood of

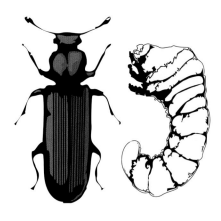

ash, hickory, oak, poplar, and walnut. Telltale signs are small ¹⁄₁₆-inch circular holes and the presence of fine, brown, flour-like wood material.

Prevention

The use of borate wood preservatives such as PeneTreat and coating the wood with a finish will help to make infestation more difficult. Make sure there are no moisture problems in the home. A finish that contains a surface insecticide like CPF-2D is also an effective deterrent to infestation.

Treatment

As a spot treatment, inject approved insecticides into holes with a glue syringe. Once insecticide has been applied, seal off tunnel entrances by pounding in wooden dowels or by using caulking, wood putty, WoodEpox, or a mixture of LiquidWood and sawdust. See more about LiquidWood and WoodEpox on pages 134–137.

Round-Headed Wood Borers

The round-headed borer adults of the family Cerambycidae are commonly called pine sawyers or long-horned beetles (shown on page 39). The old

These ¼" round holes are the telltale signs of round-headed borers. If the holes were oblong, it would signify the presence of flat-headed borers.

house borer is also a member of this family. These are some of the largest wood boring beetles in North America ranging in size from ¼ inch to 3 inches long. They are also easy to identify by their extremely long antennae which can be up to three times longer than their bodies.

They can be quite destructive, chewing through not only wood but also plasterboard, hardwood flooring, plywood, shingles, and carpeting. They do, however, prefer the sapwood of coniferous trees. Fortunately, most of the round-headed borers do not reinfest. One exception is the old house borer whose larval stage can last from two to three years or as long as 15 years, in very dry wood. The old house borer's tunnels are distinctively marked with a rippled pattern.

The black pine sawyer, also known as the white spotted sawyer *(Monochamus scutellatus)*, is one of the 1,200 species of long-horned beetles in North America.

Prevention

The use of borate wood preservatives such as PeneTreat and coating the wood with a finish will help to make infestation more difficult. Make sure there are no moisture problems in the home. A finish that contains a surface insecticide like CPF-2D is also an effective deterrent to infestation.

Treatment

As a spot treatment, inject approved insecticides into holes with a glue syringe. Once insecticide has been applied, seal off tunnel entrances by pounding in wooden dowels or by using caulking, wood putty, WoodEpox, or a mixture of LiquidWood and sawdust. See more about LiquidWood and WoodEpox on pages 134–137.

Termites

These insects can do serious damage to any wooden structure. Annually, termites cause over 2.5 billion dollars of damage affecting over 600,000 homes in the U.S. Without early detection, extensive damage can be done before the damage is even visible. Termites build tunnels through the soil looking for wood, especially moist wood that they can eat. You can easily tell the difference between winged ants and winged termites—the ants have elbowed antennae and a very narrow waist. Termites have thick waists and their antennae have a slight curve, but are not elbowed like the ants'.

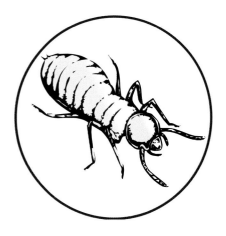

Termites form five major groups in the United States: subterranean, drywood, dampwood, powderpost, and Formosan. Subterranean termites are responsible for over 90 percent of all termite-related damage and are found in every state in the U.S. and in Canada. The drywood termites are more common in southern and coastal areas; their damage to wooden structures is the most costly to treat.

Distribution of Subterranean Termites

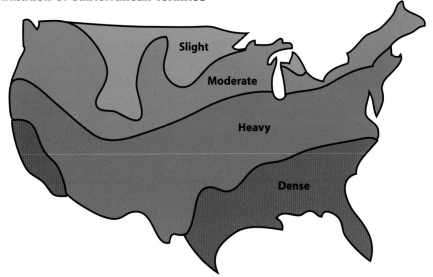

Prevention

Consult your local building codes. If you are in a termite region, most building codes require a metal termite shield under your foundation. Research has shown that sand with a 10 to 16 particle mesh has proven to be an effective termite shield. Termites cannot tunnel through a sand barrier and so are physically unable enter into your foundation.

Check for cracks that termites can enter in concrete foundations. If cracks are found, patch with cement. Make sure that no wood directly touches the soil; this includes posts, steps, boardwalk style decking, etc. Also make sure that there are no moisture problems with the wood.

Ideally, wood should be at least eight inches above the soil, but if you adhere to the 2-foot minimum suggested for sill logs mentioned in *Chapter 2: Design for Easy Maintenance* on page 13, you will be more than protected, not only from possible termite infestation but from other moisture and fungus problems as well.

Treatment

If you suspect termites have infested your log home, consult with a qualified pest control agency. Look for an agency that will charge a separate fee for both inspection and treatment of termites. Be wary of agencies that offer free inspections and then try to make their money on charging for their treatment services. Unscrupulous companies have charged unsuspecting homeowners for multiple termite treatments when in fact there were no termites present.

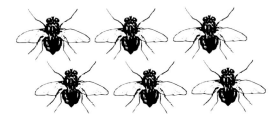

Winter Flies

You see them every year around mid to late August—flies gather around screen doors and inside windows searching for warmth. The most common of these flies is the cluster fly. These tend to be larger than the common housefly and are dark gray in color. They hibernate in the house structure (particularly around the windows) through the colder temperatures but will emerge from hibernation during warm spells. The good news about winter flies is that they are harmless to humans and will not destroy property. Also, they do not breed while indoors, despite their numbers.

Prevention

To help minimize the number of flies that can enter into your home in the fall, make sure that window and door screens are tight fitting and free of holes or tears. A finer mesh screen may be needed to prevent them from entering. Also, since flies are attracted to the warmth of a house, minimize the amount of time that doors are left open.

Treatment

The cheapest means of control is the good old fly swatter. Pest strips also work well. For large swarms, a vacuum cleaner can be used for removal of flies from screens and windows. Insecticides may also be used to control these flies, but consider if it is really worth using poison to control a harmless pest. If you decide to use insecticides, follow the instructions and cautions on the label.

Wood Wasps

These are members of the family Siricidae and are also known as horntails. They are over an inch in size and are wasp-like in appearance but lack the narrow waist that is commonly associated with both bees and wasps. The females have long ovipositors protruding from their abdomens that they use to inject eggs into wood. Once hatched, the larvae feed and tunnel through both sapwood and heartwood. Like the round-headed borers, they have the ability to chew through

plasterboard and hardwood flooring, though the damage they do is mostly cosmetic. The female lays only a few eggs at a time and they will not reinfest.

Prevention

The use of borate wood preservatives such as PeneTreat and coating the wood with a finish will help to make infestation more difficult. A finish that contains a surface insecticide like CPF-2D is also an effective deterrent to infestation.

Treatment

As a spot treatment, inject approved insecticides into holes with a glue syringe. Once insecticide has been applied, seal off tunnel entrances by pounding in wooden dowels or by using caulking, wood putty, WoodEpox, or a mixture of LiquidWood and sawdust. See more about LiquidWood and WoodEpox on pages 134–137.

Chapter 5: Log Home Pests

Besides insects, there are a number of animals that can be a nuisance to log homes. Bats, porcupines, squirrels, swallows, woodpeckers, and other birds make up the bulk of nuisance critters.

Bats seem to elicit the majority of complaints from log homeowners about problems from animals other than insects. Bat houses can be set up to provide alternate housing for bats. Birds can cause damage as well, by pecking the wood as in the case of woodpeckers, and also by nesting in and defecating down the sides of the logs. Porcupines can do considerable damage by chewing into the wood of homes.

A strategically placed bat house.

Bats

Bats are beneficial animals that consume massive amounts of beetles, caddis flies, flying ants, mayflies, mosquitoes, moths, and other insects. They can also be a nuisance to any home.

Bats can present serious health risks through pathogens that exist in accumulations of their feces in attic and soffit areas. Unpleasant odors from dead bats inside a structure and from their feces can also be a problem. Bats urinate and defecate while flying or from a stationary position and can stain and damage the exteriors of log structures (see next page).

Bats can also carry rabies, though less than 1 percent of them are infected. However, leather gloves should always be worn when handling or working around bats to reduce the risk of any possible rabies infection.

Prevention
Bats can squeeze through cracks approximately ¼ inch by 1½ inches or a hole ⅝ inch by ⅞ inch. Some of the smaller species can enter a hole the size of a dime. Install screens over chimneys and behind vents. Caulk all cracks and gaps especially around the roof and soffit areas. Make sure that doors seal tightly and that windows have screens. Placing bat houses near your home will

not automatically draw bats away from your house. The houses will, however, provide a home for them once they have been eradicated from your house so you can benefit from their insect hunting skills.

Treatment for Bat Removal

The simplest method of removing a bat from the living area of a home is to chase it into one room and then allow it to fly out through an open window. Healthy bats will not attack even when chased. An insect net will also work to capture a bat for removal from the home.

If bats are suspected in the attic or soffit areas, seal all possible cracks and crevices with caulking or wire mesh screens except the largest opening. Cut the end out of a nylon stocking and staple it snugly around the opening. This will work as a one-way valve allowing the bats to fly out but not reenter the home. The bats will eventually leave the house structure to hunt for food and will be unable to return. Once the bats have left the house, remove the stocking and properly seal the last remaining opening.

Bats nested in the logwork under the eaves and the acidity of their excrement has had a damaging, corrosive effect on the logs and finish of this structure.

Treatment for Finish Damaged by Bat Excrement

The bats will need to be eradicated from their roosting area in the logwork. Once the bats have been removed from the area, the remaining finish should be stripped away and the logs bleached with TSP to thoroughly remove discoloration and odor from logs. Refinish with a log home finish. Bird screen could be installed around the area where the bats were roosting to restrict future access.

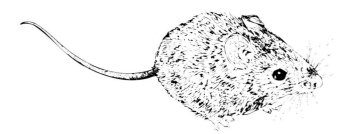

Mice

Mice too are problem pests that can cause damage to log homes. Like beaver, mice keep their paired incisor teeth which grow continuously. Gnawing or rubbing their teeth together is the only way they can keep them trimmed. Damage to logwork is done by gnawing and chewing. Electrical damage and house fires can be caused by chewing as well. Though it's not common, mice have been known to chew completely through the corner notches of log homes, allowing them to gain entry for nesting and food.

Prevention

Like bats, mice can enter the home through very small openings and so it is important to make sure that your log house is properly sealed with caulking. There is no way to aesthetically mouse proof logwork except by monitoring the logs for the sign of small teeth marks.

Keeping a clean house helps to deter mice from taking up residence. Also, keeping the area around the outside of your home free of weeds and debris will help deter mice. If birds are being fed birdseed near the house, mice will be also be attracted to the birdseed. Do not stack firewood, lumber, or other stored items near the exterior walls of your house; such items give mice a place to nest and live. An area of gravel around the perimeter of your log house

will help keep mice from burrowing near the logwork. Mechanical traps can be set outside the home to capture mice before they enter the home. Bloodmeal is also supposed to deter mice.

Treatment for Mouse Removal

Mechanical traps will work to eradicate mice. Approved poisons can also be used. The problem with poisons is that you are introducing toxins into your living space and this can be a serious problem, especially if small children are around. There is also the annoyance of a poisoned mouse dying behind a panelled or sheetrocked wall or ceiling and stinking hideously.

Mouse gnaw marks.

Treatment for Mouse Gnaw Marks

Depending on the amount, gnaw marks can either be left and then refinished later, or filled with a wood putty such as WoodEpox. See more about WoodEpox on pages 134–137.

Porcupines

Porcupines occasionally cause damage by chewing into wood surfaces. They search out salts and resins in wood, particularly in plywood and wood substrates. They have also been known to chew on the logs of log homes and cause damage, especially when a borate wood preservative has been used on the logs and not sealed by a finish. Again, it is the salts in the borates that the porcupines are trying to ingest.

Prevention

If a borate wood preservative was used on the logs, seal the logs with a log home finish. Make sure that wood substrate–type soffit material is also sealed with a finish. Fencing can also be used to minimize porcupine damage.

It is important to note that borate wood preservatives used on laminated exterior wood siding, such as T1-11 and other similar products, may cause delamination of the wood fiber sheeting. However, other wood preservatives may be used.

Treatment

Porcupines are considered nongame animals in the U.S. and are not pro-

tected. Live-trapping with large commercial cage traps or homemade box-style traps is effective.

Place the trap in the vicinity of the damage and bait with a salt-soaked cloth, sponge, or piece of wood. Once the porcupine is caught, it must be moved at least 25 miles to ensure that it will not return. Steel leghold traps (number 2 or 3) may be legal in some areas. Day shooting and spotlighting are also effective where legal. Check with your local Fish and Wildlife Service for local restrictions.

Finish chewed by porcupines.

Treatment for Finish Chewed by Porcupines

Replace damaged plywood or wood substrate materials with new, finished ones. If the damage is due to gnawing on log corner notches, a wood putty such as WoodEpox can be used to fill in the chewed areas. See more about WoodEpox on pages 134–137.

Squirrels

Squirrels can also be a nuisance. Typically, they like to find their way into the attic spaces of homes where they can nest. The attraction for them is the dry, warm, quiet atmosphere, free from predators. Once inside your home they will go to work chewing on insulation, electrical wires (causing an electrical-fire hazard), and essentially anything that they can gnaw.

Prevention

Make sure that your house is completely sealed from squirrel entry. Squirrels like to go through holes that already exist or ones that they chew themselves. Check around the roof and soffit areas particularly because this is generally where squirrels will make their entrance. Chimneys should have screens installed to keep squirrels out.

Trim back any branches that are within 20 feet of the roof of your house. Squirrels like to enter a house around the roof area; removing branches will make it more difficult for them to gain access. Also, make sure that downspouts have screens in them so that squirrels can't climb up through them to the roof. Like mice, squirrels will be attracted to birdfeed near the house.

Finish chewed by squirrels.

Treatment for Finish Chewed by Squirrels

If you own a cat or a ferret and don't mind it running around in your attic, the squirrels (as well as other critters) most definitely will. Otherwise, ultra-sonic noise devices (the type around 30–40 kHz) will work to rid attic areas of squirrels. The high frequency squeal is like a dog whistle; animals such as squirrels can hear it, but humans can't. To them the sound is like another squirrel in pain or terror, which drives them to more peaceful domains.

Another similar method is to install motion activated floodlights in the attic. Squirrels hate the bright light, and the motion-sensing switch will help keep your light bill in check. Other remedies include products similar to mothballs that repel squirrels because of odor, and live traps.

Swallows

Swallows cause problems by building nests on sides of log homes and then depositing their droppings down the length of the wall. The droppings are not only aesthetically unappealing, but if left on the logs for an extended length of time, they can damage the finish.

Prevention

Bird netting can be used to repel birds by placing it under the eaves of the home (see example on page 49). Metal repel strips such as those made by Nixalite are another way to keep unwanted birds from nesting under the eaves. The metal wire strips prevent the birds from gaining a foothold under the eaves and this forces them to look elsewhere. The Nixalite strips come in different styles for a range of different birds and critters and can be painted to match the color of your home; they are less obtrusive than the netting.

This swallow nest was built next to a metal bird repel strip. If the repel strips had continued down the length of the area, the swallows would not have nested.

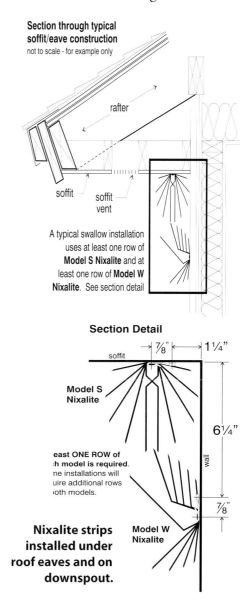

Section through typical soffit/eave construction
not to scale - for example only

rafter

soffit

soffit vent

A typical swallow installation uses at least one row of **Model S Nixalite** and at least one row of **Model W Nixalite**. See section detail

Section Detail

soffit

⅞"   1¼"

Model S Nixalite

6¼"

wall

east ONE ROW of :h model is required. ne installations will uire additional rows oth models.

⅞"

Model W Nixalite

Nixalite strips installed under roof eaves and on downspout.

Architectural "nooks" like the one shown above make perfect sites for birds to build their nests. These types of areas will have to be monitored for nest building activity or blocked off with products like Nixalite strips, screen, or netting.

Treatment

Swallows cannot lawfully be harmed. You may need a depredation permit issued by the U.S. Fish and Wildlife Service to legally remove swallow nests. Consult with your local Fish and Wildlife Service about permit requirements and restrictions. Once the swallow nests have been removed, install either the bird netting or Nixalite strips to deter future nest building.

Clean the droppings off the logs with a scrub brush, soap and water. If there is damage to the finish, touch up as needed.

Swallows cause problems by building nests on sides of log homes and then depositing their droppings down the length of the wall.

Woodpeckers

Prevention

For minimizing damage to eaves, the most effective long-term method has been the use of bird netting. The plastic netting is attached to the edge of the eaves and then angled back to the side of the house. When installed properly, the netting is barely visible from a distance (or can be spray painted to approximate the color of the home).

Treatment

Scaring woodpeckers away with the use of loud noises has been done with some success. Controlling insects also reduces the likelihood of woodpecker damage. See *Chinking Damaged by Birds* on page 69.

Woodpeckers can also be a nuisance to your log home, doing considerable damage to logs, wood siding, and chinking. Woodpeckers generally do the most damage from February through June, which is the time for territory establishment and also the breeding season.

The damage to log buildings can take several forms. Holes are often drilled in eaves, exterior log surfaces, window frames, and trim boards. Caulking and chinking between the logs is susceptible to woodpecker attacks, especially if there are insects present in the logs. Natural colored finishes and stained wood surfaces are typically preferred over painted wood.

Not only can woodpeckers do physical damage to log homes, they can also produce annoying "drumming" sounds. Drumming is the term for the rhythmic pecking of surfaces that include metal gutters and downspouts, chimney caps, TV antennas, metal roofing, and metal garbage cans.

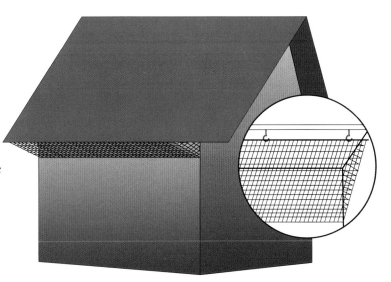

Plastic netting is shown attached from the outside edge of the eave and angled back to the siding. The insert shows a method of attaching the netting with hooks and wooden dowels.

Chapter 6: Caulking & Chinking

Backer Rod and Chinking Step-by-Step

Step 1. Select Backer Rod

Backer rod is a synthetic foam that is available in a variety of shapes and sizes from ¼ inch up to 5 inches. The reason backer rod needs to be placed in the joints is that it acts as a bond breaker, which provides a surface that chinking won't adhere to. Eventually, the chinking will free itself from the backer rod and will move with the logs as they expand or shrink. Backer rod also serves to add an insulation value and reduce the amount of chinking material needed.

The most common mistake that people make when choosing backer rod is choosing a backer that is too big for the joint. When this happens, the backer keeps coming out or you are left with a chinked joint that is larger than it needs to be. Typically, the backer rod size will be half the joint size, i.e. ½-inch backer rod for a 1-inch joint. Keep in mind that you may require a number of different styles and sizes for your particular project.

Closed Cell Backer Rod

is a closed cell polyethylene round foam that also runs in a continuous length. It is sold by the foot or by the case from ¼ inch up to 4 inch. Compared to dual rod, this backer is firm, but just as easy to install.

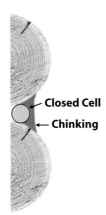

— Closed Cell
← Chinking

A blunt tool may be needed to push backer deeper into the joint to allow the required amount of chinking.

Dual Rod

is a backer rod that can be described as an open cell, extruded polyethylene foam. Dual rod is extruded to leave an impermeable shell to prevent moisture from entering the side. It is available in a continuous length through the 1⅛-inch size; larger sizes are available in 6-foot lengths. This may be sold by the foot or case, and is available from ⅜ inch to 4 inches.

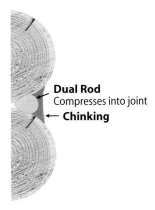

Dual Rod
Compresses into joint
← Chinking

Advantages of this backer are that it is very flexible and is easy to install, especially in smaller joints. Smaller sizes are offered to fit those really tight joints. In choosing a size, the diameter should be approximately 25 percent larger than the joint because of the compressibility. Care must be taken not to puncture or stretch it during application; this may cause outgassing. In smaller joints a blunt tool may be needed to push backer further into the joint to allow the required amount of chinking.

Grip Strip

is available in 4-foot lengths. Sizes are available from ¾ inch up to 5 inches. It provides an excellent fit with a

— Grip Strip
← Chinking

flat working surface and is a closed cell product that repels water. This material is quick and easy to use. No tools are necessary and it follows the curvature of the logs. This product really grips to the logs and stays in place.

Open Cell Backer

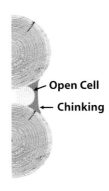

Open Cell

Chinking

Rod is very flexible and easy to work with. It is soft and compresses to fit most size joints. This product does not have a water resistant coating (it looks like a sponge in the form of a rope) making it breathable which allows for a faster cure, but it's best used in the interior. This is because it will absorb water. If used on the exterior, only put in the amount of open cell that you think will get done in one day so the exposed backer will not draw in moisture.

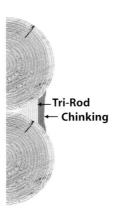

Tri-Rod

Chinking

Tri-Rod is a closed cell backing material that offers a flat working surface. This is polyethylene foam backer that is designed for round logs. It is a triangular strip and is available in 6-foot lengths.

You may need a spray adhesive such as Touch and Seal or Foam Weld to keep it in place. When installing the tri-rod around knots and curvature of the logs, the backer must be cut out on the backside. This will keep the backer from projecting out and will keep the chinking uniform. This does take more time to install.

Step 2. Review Proper and Improper Joint Design

Proper Joint Design

Backer rod is needed to serve as a bond breaker. The following illustrations graphically depict why two-point adhesion is so important for the performance of any caulk or chinking product. Caulk and chinking are designed to stretch and be flexible, but as you'll see in the illustrations, the material can fully flex to absorb log movement only if a bond breaker is installed down the center of the joint.

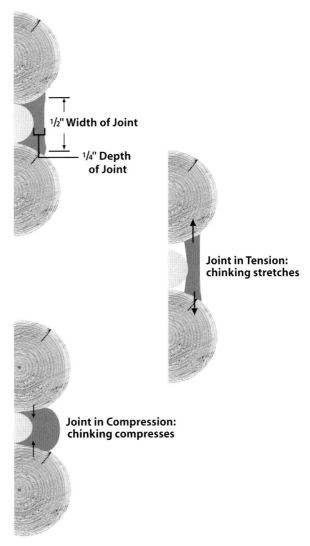

½" Width of Joint

¼" Depth of Joint

Joint in Tension: chinking stretches

Joint in Compression: chinking compresses

Improper Joint Design

When a bond breaker is not used, the chinking is adhered to the joint with three-point adhesion. Adhesive and cohesive failures occur. Cracks will appear in the chinking, opening up the possibility of water, rot, wind, and insect damage.

Joint Relaxed: chinking adhered to all 3 points

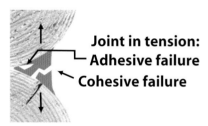

Joint in tension: Adhesive failure Cohesive failure

Step 3. Prepare Surface

For chinking to adhere properly to the logs, they must be clean and free of dirt, pollen, oils, sawdust, and other accumulated debris.

Use a leaf blower or a broom to remove from the logs cobwebs and other debris that may have accumulated. To remove fine particles of pollen, sand, and dust, wash the logs down with a damp rag or a gentle spray from a garden hose, or you can lightly power wash the logs with tap water. If you decide to power wash, use a very low setting so as not to physically damage the logs.

Use denatured alcohol or a biodegradable stripper like Super Bio-Strip to remove uncured oils, such as chain bar oil or wet sap. Mineral spirits can leave behind an oily residue that can cause

Installing GripStrip backer rod. In order to properly install, different sizes and shapes are necessary for this log wall.

possible future adhesion problems for caulking, chinking, and finishes.

Step 4. Install Backer Rod

Use your fingers to place lengths of backer rod into the log joints. Separate pieces of backer rod should fit snugly next to each other in the joint. The use of a blunt tool when installing backer rod to the exterior logs will prevent punctures to the surface of the rod and minimize blistering. You can read more about blisters on pages 60 and 76–77.

GripStrip backer rod gets its name from its ability to grip to the logs. This makes it fast and easy to apply, really taking the headache out of doing a big chinking job. Some professional applicators will use a quiver that holds a large number of different sizes of backer rod. This makes it easier to do a lot of joinery without having to make many trips back to where the backer rod is stockpiled.

If the backer rod seems to keep popping out, a smaller size or a different style of backer rod is needed. You should never have to nail or staple backer rod to keep it in place. Spray adhesives work well to help hold backer rod in place. If you use spray adhesives, be sure to spray the adhesive only on the backer rod and not on the logs. This keeps the logs clean from any debris that may adhere to the sprayed area of the logs and also minimizes extra cleanup later on.

For smaller joints where backer rod cannot fit, but yet there may be a gap, a mylar tape or packaging tape may be used. This too will serve as a bond-breaker to allow the chinking material to release itself from the tape and move with logs as they settle and shrink. A bond-breaker tape should be used if applying chinking over old mortar, as well. Packaging tape or duct tape are two examples that will work for this situation.

Before you actually start applying the chinking, read and follow the manufacturer's directions carefully. Chinking needs to be applied within a specific temperature range that varies from manufacturer to manufacturer. By following their guidelines, you can greatly minimize problems later on.

How Much Caulk or Chinking Do I Need?

There is often confusion about figuring the amount of caulk or chinking that is needed for a log home. Most homeowners know the square footage of their log homes, but unfortunately that information is not applicable for calculating caulk or chinking. To figure the amount needed, you will need to estimate the lineal footage of all of the gaps and joints you will be filling with caulk or chinking. The steps below will help you determine the amount needed based on measurements and averages that you supply.

Average Width of Joint		Lineal feet per full gallon (231 cubic inches)												
Average Depth of Joint		¼"	⅜"	½"	⅝"	¾"	⅞"	1"	1½"	2"	2½"	3"	3½"	4"
	¼"	308	205	154	123	102	88	77	51	39	31	25	22	19
	⅜"		136	102	82	68	58	51	34	25	20	17	14	13
	½"			77	61	51	44	38	25	19	15	13	11	9

Example: One full gallon is sufficient material to fill a joint ½ inch wide, ⅜ inch deep and 102 feet long.

1. Add up the total length of all of your walls and multiply that number by the average number of log courses.

2. Then, look up the lineal foot per gallon based on the average width and depth of your joint from the chart.

3. Divide the total from No. 1 by the chart number from No. 2. This will give you a quick estimate of the total gallons needed for the exterior of your log home. If you will be caulking or chinking the interior, you will need to double the amount.

To Convert Gallons to Tubes:

_____ Total gallons x 128 oz./gal. = _____ Total oz.

Then divide the Total oz. by the tube size:

_____ Total oz. ÷ Tube size in oz. (10.5 or 29) = _____ Tubes.

To Figure Cases:

10.5 (oz.) = _____ Number of tubes divided by case size = _____ cases.

29 (oz.) = _____ Number of tubes divided by case size = _____ cases.

About Finishes and Chinking

Chinking is a textured, synthetic caulking that gives the appearance of mortar. Many log homeowners prefer a contrast of colors between the chinking and finish of their homes. Applying a stain or finish prior to chinking the logs is necessary to accomplish the desired look—it is much easier to finish the logs first and then apply the chinking. Finishes for chinked homes frequently have a clear maintenance coat to ease recoating.

Make sure that both the finish and chinking that you have chosen are compatible with one another. Not all log home finishes are compatible with all chinking products. Finishes that contain waxes and stearates can cause adhesion problems with some caulking and chinking products.

If you are using products from a company that manufactures both chinking and finishes, this is not a concern. If you are using products from two different manufacturers, inquire about compatibility issues.

If in doubt, remember that polyurethane based caulk or chinking will adhere to practically all log finishes on the market, though it is more expensive and is more difficult to apply then latex based caulk and chinking material.

Chinking and Application Tools

Bulk loading gun and follow plate.

Chinking is packaged in 5-gallon pails and quart tubes. For big jobs, 5-gallon pails are more economical.

When using 5-gallon pails, chinking can be applied by troweling, with grout bags, with a bulk loading caulk gun and follow plate, or with a commercial chink pump system. The pump systems dispense chinking in a smooth, continuous flow, making it very fast and easy to apply.

One such device is the Snorkler from Sashco. This machine is designed primarily for professional chinking applicators and allows handling of bulk quantities of chinking material. Homeowners may rent the Snorkler or chink pumps through chinking retailers.

The Sascho Snorkler.

The most common set of tools for homeowners working with 5-gallon quantities is a bulk loading gun and a follow plate. The follow plate makes for quick reloading of the bulk gun for faster application time at a minimal cost. See *How to Use a Follow Plate* on the next page.

If you are not using the follow plate, place the end of the gun down into the chinking material about 2 or 3 inches and pull up on the push rod to fill. Using your index finger, scrape material off the gun until it is clean, and then wipe your finger. This helps reduce mess. It is always advisable to have a small 5-quart pail of water and a cloth handy for cleanup after each filling.

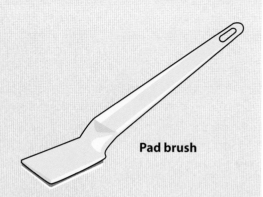

Pad brush

Tooling Equipment

Polyethylene foam brushes are available in hardware stores and lumber yards but you can also use rubber spatulas, paint brushes, putty knives, and trowels. The pad brush with removable foam pads also works very well.

A pail of clean water, clean rags, and a spray bottle filled with clean water will also be needed. To speed up the tooling process, have several sizes of foam brushes or pads on hand. When one of them picks up too much chinking and drags or smears the chinking instead of gliding over the surface, throw it into the pail of water and continue on with a clean brush or pad.

Nozzles

There are a variety of different sized nozzles available in both round and slot styles. For smaller beads, a round style nozzle works well; but for wider joints the slot style nozzles are much more efficient.

When choosing a nozzle size, be aware that the depth of the bead of caulk should be half the size of the width of the joint, but never thinner than ¼ inch or thicker than ½ inch; for example, for a joint 1 inch wide the bead depth should be ⅜ inch to ½ inch.

To slow latex chinking from setting up too quickly while you work, a mixture of 1 part denatured alcohol and 2 parts water can be used to spray over the chinking when the temperature is over 70 degrees.

How to Use a Follow Plate

Remove the front cap of the caulk gun, and then wet the end of gun with water or a release agent. A mixture of 50 percent water and 50 percent denatured alcohol makes a good release agent.

Spray or pull water up into the gun chamber to help lubricate the interior. Then, place the follow plate inside the pail and on top of the caulk or chinking. Seat the plate firmly. This will keep bubbles from forming inside the gun as you fill it.

Attach the caulk gun to the plate and lock the push rod locking mechanism; pull up slowly until the gun is full. Unscrew the gun from the plate and reattach the front cap.

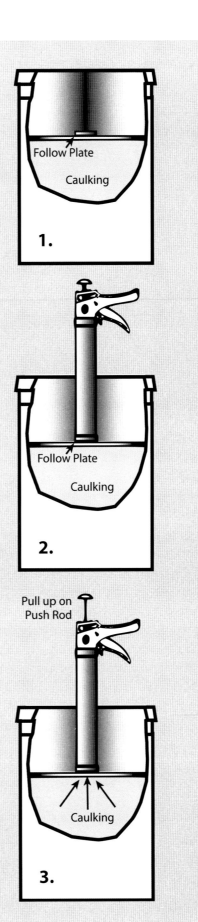

Backer Rod & Chinking Step-by-Step

Also make sure not to apply the chinking when it is early in the morning or in the evening when temperatures are too cool to allow the chinking to have proper adhesion to the log surfaces. In excessive heat (90 degrees or more), application during the morning or evening may be necessary.

Step 6. Pack Chinking for Adhesion

Using a damp polyethylene foam brush or pad brush, holding the foam portion parallel to the bead, gently press the bead into place. A small plastic bucket of water is handy to have nearby for keeping the brush damp and clean of any built-up chinking.

You don't want to drag the foam brush down the bead but instead press the foam brush against the bead, section by section. This packs the chinking against the backer rod and the upper and

Step 5. Application

Apply the chinking material over the backer rod and along the center of the joint. Be sure that some of the chinking material overlaps slightly onto the surface of both the upper and lower logs. When you first attempt the application process, try starting out with about three feet of chinking. This will give you a good amount of practice area, which you can reasonably tool out before it starts to set up and skin over. As you become more comfortable with tooling the material, you will be able to apply longer beads and work more quickly.

The weather is going to impact how much chinking you will be able to apply. If it is very sunny or breezy, the chinking will set up faster and you will really have to hustle to pack it and tool it out smoothly.

Packing the chinking to ensure adhesion.

lower sides of the logs, ensuring proper adhesion to the logs as well as providing a uniform density to the chinking. The next step is the actual tooling or smoothing out of the chinking surface.

Step 7. Tooling the Chinking

Using the spray bottle, lightly mist the chinking with water to allow the brush to glide over the surface. If you are using a latex chinking like Log Jam, Perma-Chink, or 1010 chinking and the temperature is over 70 degrees, a mixture of 1 part denatured alcohol and 2 parts water can be used. When working in temperatures below 70 degrees, the alcohol is not needed; just mist with water.

Do not apply too much water, or the latex chinking will become oversaturated and start to run down the logs, making a mess. If this happens, just wipe off with a damp sponge or rag. Be sure to have plenty of clean rags available, especially if you have never applied chinking before.

If you are using polyurethane based caulk or chinking product like Manus-Bond or Sika Flex, any water that is applied will actually speed up the curing process of the product. To avoid this, straight alcohol only should be used when tooling, unless, of course, you want to speed up the cure time.

The polyurethane based products tend to be stickier than their latex based counterparts and you may find them to be more of a challenge to tool. You may want to practice tooling the polyurethane based products on scrap wood or on a smaller section of log joinery. Try a 1-foot length to get started, to keep it manageable until you get the

Tooling chinking.

hang of it and feel comfortable with taking on an entire house.

The idea of tooling is simply to smooth out any ripples caused when the chinking was applied. One of the important aspects of tooling is to feather the bead of chinking out to the top and bottom logs at least ¼ inch.

Many people are tempted to use their fingers to tool out chinking but this should be avoided. Convex instruments (like fingers) will push the chinking away from the center of the joint, causing a thin area in the middle. It is best to use a flat tool to keep a uniform amount of chinking over the backer rod.

Some Notes about Blisters

Blisters are a phenomenon commonly found after applying chinking. They form when moisture from the chinking accumulates in voids beneath the bead of chinking and the heat from the sun causes water vapor to expand, causing a blister to appear as a "bubble" in the chinking.

To avoid these blisters, use a white tarp to shield freshly chinked walls from the sun. If this is not possible, keep a close eye on the chinked wall for the first 24 to 48 hours.

If a blister pops up, just puncture a hole in the middle of it and gently push the chinking back into place. Then after three to five days you can repair the blister by applying a small portion of chinking material into the hole. Read more about blisters on page 76–77.

Cure Time

When the chinking process is finished, allow chinking to cure for one week if you will be finishing the logs with oil or latex stains and finishes. The total

cure-through time is approximately one month for most products. However, check with the literature that came with the product for specific guidelines.

In areas where autumn nighttime temperatures fall below freezing, protect the newly applied chinking with a plastic tarp. In extremely cold conditions, insulation board can be used.

To keep the curious from leaving finger marks in the fresh chinking, consider hanging a small board with several beads of the chinking in a conspicuous area with a sign inviting people to satisfy their curiosity.

Step 8.
Cleanup and Disposal

To properly dispose of unused chinking material, it is good practice to understand and follow all of your state and local regulations on cleanup and disposal.

Synthetic chinking is latex based and the cleanup should be handled much in the same way as that of latex (water-based) paints.

Do not dispose of chinking material in drinking water supplies. However, for easy cleanup water may be used for cleaning hands, surfaces and equipment. Toxic solvents are not normally required for chinking material cleanup unless you choose to use a urethane based caulking.

Care of Bulk Loading Guns

A bulk loading caulk gun will provide you with good service if you keep it clean and lubricated. The trick is to take the time and thoroughly clean it at the end of your chinking project.

Cleanup

If chinking continues from day to day, the gun can be placed in a plastic garbage bag to keep air from curing the chinking. When finished at the end of the job, put any remaining caulk or chinking back into the pail and seal it tightly. Then place the gun into a pail of clean water with the cap removed and pull up on the push rod to suck water up into the gun. Keep doing this until the gun is clean of material.

Once the gun is clean, spray a light lubricant like WD-40 into gun chamber. Also unscrew the trigger mechanism and spray WD-40 into the back. Leave the gun open until it is dry. This will help keep the interior from rusting. Also be sure to wipe the exterior with a light oil.

Other Maintenance

If the gun is not maintained and a buildup of caulk or chinking material develops on or in the gun, you can remove it by first soaking with brush and roller cleaner. After the material has softened, the interior of the gun can be cleaned with a 2-inch or 3-inch wire wheel attached to a ¼-inch drill extension.

Other Troubleshooting

If the gun will not fill, the leathers are probably either worn or dried out. With the leathers still in the gun, place the end of the gun in warm water and keep pulling up on the push rod until water is pulled up and into the gun chamber. If you are working in the fall, the material may be cold and leaking fluid. Either keep the material in a heated space or place the pail of caulk or chinking material in a tub of heated water.

If the leathers are buckled, the leathers will lose shape if stored or soaked in water for too much time. Replace the leathers as needed.

A maintained gun will give you a much better chinking and caulking experience, so do clean it daily; and if you cannot because of an emergency, place the whole gun in a plastic bag and seal it up until you can take the time to thoroughly clean it.

By thoroughly caulking all log joinery, cracks, and crevices you can reduce heat loss and protect against water infiltration and rot.

Caulking a Log Home

Caulking a log home is an important step in sealing log joinery and other cracks and crevices from the elements, reducing heat loss, and preventing insect infestation.

There are many different brands of caulking on the market to choose from, some performing better than others. Be aware that there are quality caulking compounds made specifically for log homes, formulated in a variety of popular colors to enhance the colors of stains and finishes of log homes.

Caulking for log homes is available in two different formulations, latex based and polyurethane based.

Latex based caulking such as LogBuilder is the most common formulation found for log homes and comes in the widest variety of colors. It tends to be less expensive than polyurethane based caulking.

Polyurethane based caulking such as Manus-Bond 75-AM cures to a stronger, heavier consistency and is of a higher density than the latex caulks. It also tends to be more insect resistant and a little more expensive. It is also more difficult to tool and smooth out due to being very sticky and faster-setting than latex caulking. Unlike the latex caulks that stay damp when water is sprayed or misted on the uncured surface, polyurethane caulking will actually set up and skin over more quickly when misted with water. This can be an advantage or disadvantage depending on your situation when applying.

Decks that butt directly next to exterior log walls should be caulked to seal off water from seeping in between sill logs and the foundation. On some log homes, the deck is inset into the logs or log siding and should also be caulked to seal from water and insects. Check the condition of the caulking to be sure that cracks have not developed or that it has not lost adhesion and started to pull away from either the deck or the logwork.

For instance, if you have applied latex caulking and it starts to rain or sprinkle just after you have finished, you will need to cover the caulking (or chinking) with a plastic tarp. Tack the plastic tarp at the top of the log walls so that it can drape over the logs (this can be problematic on the windward or gable ends of the home); otherwise the rainwater will wash the caulking down the logs, leaving a mess and a job that will have to be redone later on.

If you use polyurethane caulking in the same situation, the rain will cause the caulking to skin over and set quickly with no chance of it s and washing down the sides

Never use a silicone based ca for log homes. This type of caulki

adheres poorly to the log surfaces, breaks down quickly, and would have to be removed and reapplied on an on-going basis.

When caulking a log home, b seal all checks, cracks, and along the gable ends, r windows, exterior Thermal imag to scan th for hea seal

Caulking & Chinking Problem Solving

Log Check Needs Caulking

As logs dry, cracks or "checks" will open up, allowing both insects and water in. Once inside the log, water can migrate through other checks and fissures. In some cases, the water can come out on the inside of the house, dripping down the walls and causing severe water damage to the wood. If the water settles inside the log and is unable to dry out it will cause the logs to start rotting.

Insects also have free rein once inside the log and are typically attracted to moist wood. Wind and dust can enter into the house in a similar fashion, causing cold drafts and higher heating bills, as well as a dusty house.

Treatment

A powdered borate product such as PeneTreat or Timbor can be either sprinkled into the check, or mixed with water and made into a paste, then forced into the check to protect the log from any rot that might be taking place. If the check is deeper than ¼ inch, use a closed cell backer rod for filler. If the check is near a corner notch and too small to caulk, drill a small hole into the check to apply borates and fill with caulking.

When the log surface is thoroughly dry, seal the check completely with a quality log home caulking such as Conceal, Log Builder, or Manus Bond 75-AM. Silicone based caulking or other inexpensive caulkings are not recommended because they are not chemically engineered for this type of application and will lack the adhesion and elasticity necessary as the log checks expand and contract.

Horizontal Log Joint Needs Sealing

This too is a serious condition and should be attended to as soon as possible to minimize future damage. Like the log check, log joints that are open and unsealed allow insects, water, and cold drafts to enter the logwork and the house.

Prevention

Make sure that all of the exterior log joints are either caulked or chinked.

Quality construction is necessary to ensure that the log joinery is tightly fitted and constructed so that the joinery won't hang up and pull apart as the house settles.

Also, a yearly inspection of the condition of the logs, caulk, chinking, and finish will minimize the chance of problems developing later on.

Treatment

A powdered borate product such as PeneTreat or Timbor can be either sprinkled into the joint, or mixed with water and made into a paste, then forced into the joint. This protects the logs from any rot that might be taking place and will help to protect against insect infestation.

If the joint is deeper than ¼ inch, use a closed cell backer rod as a filler and bond breaker. Next, when the log surface is thoroughly dry, seal the joint with a high quality latex or urethane log home caulking or chinking. Silicone based caulking is not recommended for use on the joinery of log homes.

Vertical Log Joint Needs Sealing

This example shows the result of poor craftsmanship of a kit home that was assembled. Instead of the log ends butting up flush to the doorframe, they are unevenly cut and poorly matched to the frame. The uneven spaces must be caulked or chinked to seal out water, insects, and cold drafts.

Prevention
When kit homes are assembled, the premilled logs need to be measured properly and butted tightly together. The old carpenter's saying "Measure twice and cut once" also applies to log construction.

Treatment
A powdered borate product such as PeneTreat or Timbor can be mixed with water and made into a paste, then forced into the open spaces. This protects the logs and doorframing from any rot that might be taking place and will help to protect against insect infestation.

Another alternative is to install impel rods into the door jambs. Impel rods will protect the wood from future rot if the sealing fails and the joinery begins to collect water. See more about impel rods on pages 138–139.

Use a closed cell backer rod as a filler and bond breaker in the spaces that are ¼ inch deep or deeper. When the log surface is thoroughly dry, seal the spaces with a quality log home caulking or chinking.

Window Trim Needs Caulking

The area around this window was not sealed with caulking or chinking. Water and insects can enter into the logwork around the trim and begin to cause problems.

Treatment

A powdered borate product such as PeneTreat or Timbor can be mixed with water and made into a paste, then forced into the joint. This protects the logs from any rot that might be taking place and will help to protect against insect infestation.

If the space between the logwork and the window and trim area is deeper than ¼ inch, use a closed cell backer rod as a filler and bond breaker. Next, when the log surface is thoroughly dry, seal the areas around the trim with a quality log home caulking or chinking such as Log Builder, Log Jam, or Manus Bond 75-AM. On gable and windward sides use flashing and then caulk as a backup.

Silicone based caulking or other inexpensive caulkings are not recommended because they are not chemically engineered for this type of application and will lack the adhesion and elasticity necessary as the logs naturally expand and contract.

Chinking Damaged by Insects

These small, uniform holes are likely indications of insects boring through the caulk or chinking material. Insects are either boring into the surface to nest or they have hatched from nesting cavities within the logs and are boring their way out. Insects are usually attracted to moist and/or rotting wood. Carpenter bees, however, will bore directly into dry, healthy wood (see page 35).

Treatment

The insect infestation of the logs needs to be treated first. Look for other small holes (accompanied by fine sawdust) in the logwork. Using a syringe, inject the holes with an approved insecticide like CPF-2D. Plug the holes with caulking, WoodEpox, or a mixture of wood glue and sawdust. For more information on the prevention and treatment of insects see *Chapter 4: Insects* starting on page 30.

Once the insect problem has been dealt with, fill holes with similar caulk or chinking to seal them from future infestation and moisture infiltration.

Unlike mortar chinking, synthetic caulk and chinking will adhere perfectly to old caulk or chinking as long as the surface is dry and free of dust and debris. Apply a small amount of new chinking over the holes and spread out with a foam brush to form a seamless patch.

Monitor the chinking and logs over the next few months to see if any more holes materialize. If so, repeat the treatment until they stop appearing.

Chinking Damaged by Birds

In this photo, you can see where birds have pecked irregularly shaped holes into the latex chinking looking for insects, and even where they damaged the backer rod.

Birds can hear the insects moving within the logwork and they try to reach them. The insects have either found within the logs soft, moist wood to nest in and hatch their young or are feeding on the wood itself.

Treatment

The insect infestation of the logs needs to be treated first. Look for other small holes (accompanied by fine sawdust) in the logwork. Using a syringe, inject the holes with an approved insecticide such as CPF-2D. Plug the holes with caulking or a mixture of wood glue and sawdust. For more information on the prevention and treatment of insects see *Chapter 4: Insects* starting on page 30.

Once the insect problem has been dealt with, fill holes with similar caulk or chinking to seal them from future infestation and moisture infiltration.

Unlike mortar chinking, synthetic caulk and chinking will adhere perfectly to old caulk or chinking as long as the surface is dry and free of dust and debris. Apply a small amount of new chinking over the holes and spread out with a foam brush to form a seamless patch.

Monitor the chinking and logs over the next few months to see if any more holes materialize. If so, repeat the treatment until they stop appearing. Typically, once the insect problem has been effectively dealt with, the birds will leave the chinking alone.

Caulk or Chinking Stretched and Torn from Settling Logs

In this example, caulking was applied to the side of a stationary wall and to green logs. As the logs settled, the caulking stretched as much as it was able before losing adhesive and elastometric capacities. This is a common occurrence when caulking or chinking is used in this manner with green logs.

It should be noted that the caulking is not at fault in this situation. It simply was stretched farther than it was engineered for. It is important for the log homeowner to be aware that green logs (logs containing 20 percent or more moisture) will settle.

It is best to wait for the logs to settle before caulking is done in these areas. Settling typically takes a year.

Treatment
A putty knife can be used to scrape off the existing caulking or chinking and then new caulking can be applied. The logs shown are on the exterior of the house and are protected by a wide overhang. Because of this, the caulking could be left as is until the logs have fully settled (6 inches to 8 inches, depending on the size of the logs). Then, the logs could be cleaned up and recaulked.

Caulking or Chinking Stretched and Torn #2

Here, caulking was hastily applied to the log joints (essentially just smeared on using a finger). As the logs naturally expanded and contracted through the season, the caulking lost adhesion and pulled away from the logs. The reason the caulking lost adhesion is that it was applied too thinly.

Treatment

The caulking needs to be completely removed and new caulking applied. In order for caulking or chinking to have adequate adhesion, it should be applied with a **depth of joint** of ½ inch to ¼ inch. The corresponding **width of joint** should be between ¼ inch and 2 inches, and four times the anticipated movement of the logs (see cross section). Care should also be taken that the caulking is applied in a uniform manner and completely sealed along the log surfaces.

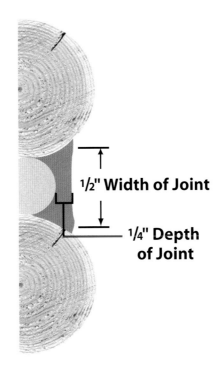

½" Width of Joint

¼" Depth of Joint

Caulking or Chinking Stretched and Torn #3

In this example, adequate adhesion of the caulking has been obtained at the log surfaces but the middle part of the chink joint has been applied too thinly (less than ¼ inch), allowing the chinking to break and tear away in the middle of the joint. Open tears like this one will allow rainwater to infiltrate the log joint and begin rotting the log from the inside out.

Prevention

When applying caulk or chinking, be sure that the material is applied at the proper thickness (at least ¼ inch). A common mistake is to use your finger as a tooling instrument for caulking and chinking. The finger tends to scoop the material more than spread it, leaving a thinner application in the center of the joint. Too much water applied while tooling the chinking can also cause adhesion problems later on.

Also, be sure to take your time when tooling out caulk or chinking. The main goal is to properly seal the log

joints, and a hurried work pace can work against that goal.

Treatment

The length of chinking that has torn will need to be removed. A razor knife or PipeKnife like the one shown can be used to cut out areas of chinking and you can typically pull out the remaining chinking with your hands. Cover the log wall loosely with a tarp to keep rain from entering the log joints.

Once the chinking has been removed, powdered borates (such as PeneTreat or Timbor) can be sprinkled into the open joint to help counteract any log rot that has taken place, and to disrupt any insects that may have entered. Make sure that there is a backer rod or other bond breaker in place for joints deeper than ¼ inch. Log surfaces and joint should be dry before reapplying chinking.

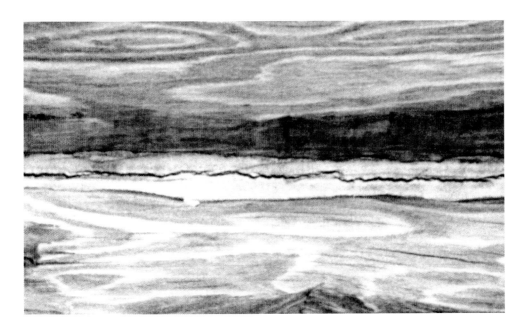

Caulking or Chinking Stretched and Torn #4

In this case, the log joint was deeper than ¼ inch and backer rod was not used. What happens is this: the logs will naturally expand and contract and since there is no bond breaker to allow the chinking to stretch in the middle (you can review why you need a bond breaker on page 50), the caulking or chinking cracks in the center.

Treatment

Depending on the condition of the caulk or chinking, the material could be completely torn out, backer rod installed, and then caulk or chinking reapplied. An alternative to removing all of the material is to run a length of packing tape down the middle of the joint, over the chinking material as shown (the tape will act as a bond breaker). Then cover the old caulking and packaging tape with a new layer of caulk or chinking.

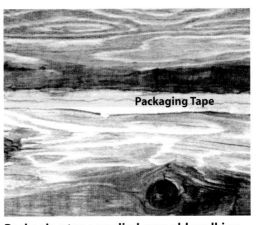

Packaging tape applied over old caulking. The tape acts as a bond breaker.

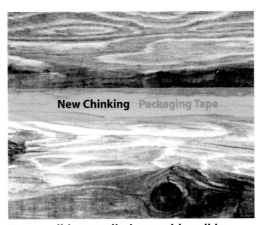

New caulking applied over old caulking and packaging tape.

Caulking or Chinking Stretched and Torn #5

Here, a type of caulking was used that did not have the elasticity necessary for log homes. Because the caulking could not stretch, the lower portion lost adhesion and peeled off the lower log. Water then entered the area and mold started to grow in and around the joint.

Prevention

When caulking a log home, be sure to use a log home caulk. Though they can cost more than other types of caulking, they are specially formulated to work with log homes. When caulking and chinking, make sure that the material is compatible with the log finish that you are using. Also, be sure to follow the manufacturer's guidelines for application.

Treatment

Remove the area of caulk or chinking that has pulled away. Use a mixture of 1 part bleach to 5 parts water to kill and clean up the mold. Rinse the area thoroughly with water. Lightly sand the log surface where the mold discoloration has taken place, then touch up with finish.

A powdered borate product such as PeneTreat or Timbor can be sprinkled into the joint or mixed with water and made into a paste, then forced into the joint. This protects the logs from any rot that might be taking place.

If the joint is deeper than ¼ inch, use a closed cell backer rod as a filler and bond breaker. When the log surface is thoroughly dry, seal the joint with a quality log home caulking or chinking such as 1010, Log Builder, Log Jam, Manus Bond 75-AM, or Perma-Chink.

Silicone based caulking is not recommended for logwork and should not be used.

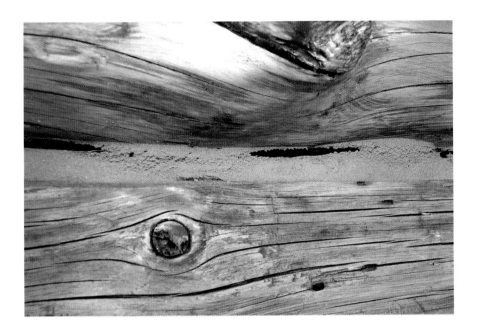

Caulking or Chinking Stretched and Torn #6

In this situation, the proper type of chinking was used, but was not applied thickly enough (less than ¼ inch thick) to the upper portion of the log. As the logs naturally expanded and contracted, the chinking tore away at the thinnest part.

Prevention

When applying chinking, make sure that there is at least ¼ inch of chinking material over the backer rod. Also be sure that if the joints are deeper than ¼ inch, a backer rod is used.

Treatment

You can chink over the existing chinking; just be sure that there is backer rod or another type of bond breaker used (if the joint is deeper than ¼ inch) and that the thickness of the new chinking is at least ¼ inch thick.

Another option is to remove the area of caulk or chinking that has pulled away. If the joint is deeper than ¼ inch, make sure that a closed cell backer rod is used as a filler and bond breaker.

When the log surface is thoroughly dry, reseal the joint with a quality log home caulking or chinking such as 1010, Log Builder, Log Jam, Manus Bond 75-AM, or Perma-Chink.

Silicone based caulking is not recommended for logwork and should not be used.

Blistering of Caulking or Chinking

Blisters typically occur right after a log home has been chinked or caulked and while the material is still soft, but has a skin formed over it.

Blistering occurs when gas (usually in the form of water vapor) becomes trapped behind the caulking or chinking, and then the heat of direct sunlight turns the moisture into water vapor. As the water vapor expands, it forms a blister in the caulk or chinking material.

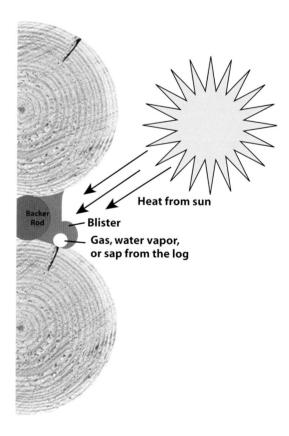

Heat from sun

Backer Rod

Blister

Gas, water vapor, or sap from the log

Possible Causes of Trapped Gas

1. An open cell backer rod was used on the exterior side of the wall that absorbed moisture.

2. A closed cell backer rod was used and was either nailed or stapled in place, or had a crack or indentation. The crack, indentation, or puncture of the closed cell material absorbed moisture. A gas used in the manufacture of the closed cell foam can leak from the backer rod through punctures. This is called outgassing.

3. A crack in the log (behind the caulking or chinking) absorbed moisture or the crack contained pitch or sap; these can also expand when heated by direct sunlight.

Prevention

Heat and water are essentially the main causes of blisters, so it is important to control the exposure of the log walls to heat or sunlight while chinking. Avoid chinking in direct sunlight, especially during the hottest time of the day. Chink on the shaded, cool side of the home. If the house has little or no shade, protect the log walls with a light-colored cloth or plastic tarp. Remember to allow room for ventilation.

Though rare, it is possible that excessive heat can build up inside the house and so it is important to be aware of the inside temperature of the house and to open a few windows if heat seems excessive.

You can also control the type of backer rod as well as how you handle the material. Avoid denting or puncturing closed cell backer rod. Using a blunt instrument to push the rod into the joints can help minimize puncturing. When applied correctly, backer rod should not have to be stapled in place. Choosing a variety of backer rod thicknesses to fit irregular joint sizes will eliminate the need for stapling and puncturing the backer rod altogether.

It is true that open cell backer rod will not cause outgassing and can be used in exterior walls, but the open cell foam will absorb water like a sponge. Generally, open cell backer rod is only recommended for interior walls or walls that will not come in contact with heavy moisture or backsplashing. Open cell backer rod is fine to use, however, if your log home is in a hot and arid climate.

It is difficult to control the pitch or sap of a log—or more specifically, where it will exit from the log. Because of this, it is recommended that you finish the logs first to seal up small cracks and fissures in the logs that may contain sap. Be sure to check the compatibility of the chinking or caulking with the finish.

Treatment of Blisters on Newly Applied Chinking

If blisters are found within the first day of chinking, you can puncture the blistered area and allow the gas to escape. Push the chinking material back to seal the punctured area. This can mar the chinked surface; if that happens, wait two to three days for the chinking to set up and then smooth over the punctured area with a small amount of fresh chinking.

Treatment of Blisters on Chinking That Has Set Up

If blisters are found on chinking that has cured more thoroughly, the blistered area will need to be cut out and removed. Next, chinking should be applied to the cavity, filling it only one-fourth to one-half of the way up. If the cause of the original blister is still present, the new chinking may push out to form a shallow blister. This can be allowed to dry and then covered up completely with new chinking.

Mortar-Based Chinking Needs Repair

Traditional mortar-based chinking will eventually crack (as shown on the top of the next page), loosen from the joint, and fall out. If you want to keep the traditional mortar chinking, you can repair it by replacing the entire length of joint with new mortar. Keep in mind that the mortar will loosen in time and have to be continually maintained. A longer lasting repair option is to use a synthetic chinking.

Treatment 1.
Repair with Synthetic Chinking

Remove all loose and crumbling chinking. Install a backer rod in the open gaps where mortar chinking was removed as shown below. Cover existing mortar chinking with plastic

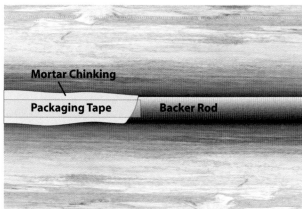

Backer rod installed in areas where mortar chinking has fallen out or been removed. Packaging tape is shown applied over mortar chinking.

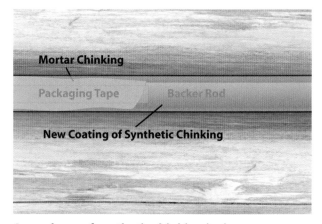

A new layer of synthetic chinking is shown applied over backer rod, mortar chinking, and tape.

Mortar chinking that has cracked and needs repair.

packaging tape (the tape will act as a bond breaker for the new synthetic chinking). Then, apply new synthetic chinking over the backer rod, packing tape, and existing mortar as shown at the bottom of page 78. The new layer of chinking should be at least ¼ inch at the thickest part.

Treatment 2.
Repair with BrushOver
Another option is to cover the mortar chinking and synthetic chinking patches with a product called BrushOver. This product can be brushed on like paint, but dries to look like new synthetic chinking.

Treatment 3.
Repair with Mortar Chinking
For those of you who want to keep the traditional mortar chinking for historical or nostalgic purposes, remove all loose and crumbling chinking along the entire length of the log. (Patch jobs next to old chinking will always crack

at the chinking-to-chinking seam and there is always a noticeable difference between old and new mortar.)

Three Mortar Chinking Recipes

Parts (Volume)	Material
1	Portland cement
1.4–8	lime
7–10	sand
¼	cement
2.1	lime
4	sand
⅛	dry pigment
⅛	excelsior
	or
	hog bristles
6	sand
3.4	lime
1	cement

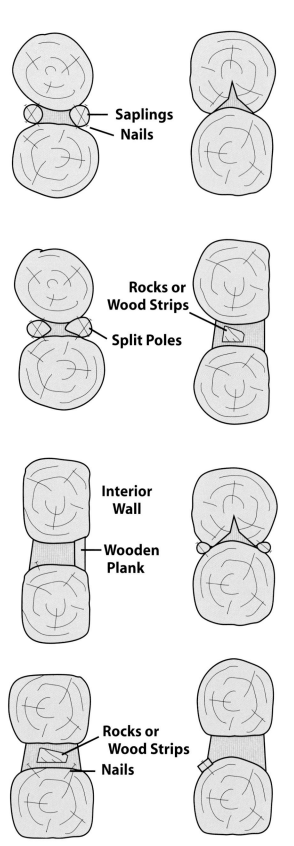

Saplings
Nails

Rocks or
Wood Strips

Split Poles

Interior
Wall

Wooden
Plank

Rocks or
Wood Strips

Nails

Above: Traditional mortar chinking techniques. If nails or wood or rock blocking is used, it should be covered with ½ inch of chinking.

Replace any damaged wood blocking with similar size material. Mix up enough mortar to be used within 30 minutes. Mix mortar thoroughly (three recipes are listed on page 79).

The consistency of the mortar should be similar to mashed potatoes. Spray a small amount of water into the joint before applying mortar. This helps keep the mortar from setting up too quickly which can cause the mortar to crack.

Using a mason's trowel, apply the mortar into the joint to a depth of 1 inch to 1½ inches thick in one continuous motion. Do not overlap layers of wet mortar; this will cause cracking and premature breakdown later on.

Angle the face of the mortar joint so that the top of the chinking is recessed farther in than the bottom of the chinking. This will help to shed water down and away from the logs and chinked joints.

Smooth the surface of the chinking with the trowel until it is slightly wet; this will give the chinking surface a smooth, glazed finish that will help repel water.

Deep or wide joints may need two or three layers of mortar so that the chinking doesn't droop and pull away from the joint. If the mortar droops because the mix is too wet or too thick, wait about 30 minutes and then re-trowel.

If applying multiple layers, the first layer should be scratched and allowed to set up. The second or final layers should be a minimum of ¾ inch thick.

Gaps in Mortar Chinking

In this example, the logs have dried out and shrunken away from the mortar based chinking. This is a common occurrence when chinking green logs with mortar. The mortar does not stretch like synthetic chinking will, and the gaps that open allow insects and water to enter into the log joinery.

Prevention

Due to its unflexing nature, mortar chinking will eventually form gaps and cracks as the logs naturally expand and contract. The only way to avoid this condition is to use backer rod and synthetic chinking instead of mortar chinking.

Treatment 1.
Repair with Synthetic Chinking

Remove all loose and crumbling chinking. Install a backer rod in the areas where mortar chinking was removed. If the open gaps where the logs shrank away from the chinking are more than ¼ inch, use a backer rod to fill the space.

Cover existing mortar chinking with plastic packaging tape (the tape will act as a bond breaker for the new synthetic chinking). Then, apply latex chinking over the backer rod, packaging tape, and existing mortar as shown on page 78.

Treatment 2.
Repair with Mortar Chinking

If you want to maintain the traditional mortar chinking, the entire row of chinking needs to be removed and replaced. Follow the same procedure as **Treatment 3** on pages 79–80.

Fabric Chinking Falling Out of Joints

Historically, chinking was essentially a two-part process consisting of "chinks" and "daubing." Chinks typically took the form of small rocks and pieces of wood that were fitted between the wall logs, filling the bulk of the open space. Daubing was a mixture of mud and straw that was used to cover the chinks.

Once the chinks were in place, the daubing mixture was applied over them to fill in the rest of the space. When the daubing had dried, a coating of whitewash was often applied to seal the daubing and provide a clean appearance.

This two-part chinking method was not strictly adhered to. People would often use whatever they could find to fill the gaps between logs. Material such as moss, mud and straw, dried cow dung, oakum, wood saplings, or pieces of old fabric twisted into ropes were used. As time went on cement mortar became a common material, to be replaced years later with polypropylene backer rod acting as the chinks and synthetic chinking acting as the daubing.

Treatment

Remove all fabric material and check for signs of rot in the log joints. If rot is present, treat with a borate wood preservative like PeneTreat. Install backer rod and chinking. See *Backer Rod & Chinking Step-by-Step* starting on page 50.

Above, an example of wood chinking made from long thin saplings. The bark is an attractive home for insects. Below is an example of the old style of daubing.

Chapter 7: Log Home Finishes

About Log Home Finishes

In order for a finish to be considered a quality log home finish, it needs to successfully perform well in five areas.

1. Provide UV Protection
2. Provide Rot Resistance
3. Provide Water Repellency
4. Provide a Flexible Finish
5. Provide a Breathable Finish

Provide UV Protection

This is necessary for providing longevity and minimizing structural breakdown of the finish. UV protection is provided through special additives which add additional cost to the finish. Clear finishes offer little if any UV protection while the pigment in colored finishes adds additional UV protection.

Provide Rot Resistance

This is taken care of mainly by the water repellency of the finish, but it should be noted that there are a number of log home finishes on the market that have borates and other preservatives added to the finish to help protect against both rot and insect attacks. Also, there are stain additives such as CPF-2D, an insecticide that can be added to the exterior finish (usually just the final coat) to help further protect against insects. Products such as CPF-2D are considered contact insecticides and work by poisoning the insects as they come in contact with the insecticide. It is important to note that these types of insecticides should never be used on interior surfaces.

Provide Water Repellency

This is directly related to rot resistance and is necessary to minimize the possibility of water damage and damaging fungal infestations. It is important to mention that a log finish can look okay and still have little or no water repellency left. You can test this by splashing a little water on different areas of the logs. The water should bead up and run off. If the water spreads out and just soaks into the surface, the water repellency is gone.

Provide a Flexible Finish

The reason this is important is that non-flexible finish coatings are less breathable and are prone to cracking and chipping as the logs naturally expand and contract. Also, flexibility aids in covering small cracks and fissures that develop in the log surface as the wood expands and contracts.

Provide a Breathable Finish

Non-breathable finishes trap moisture inside the logs, and the trapped moisture becomes an environment for mold, mildew, and other fungi to grow and rot the wood. Quality finishes allow the wood to breathe while maintaining a water repellent surface. This is possible because moisture vapor molecules are smaller than water molecules. The finish acts like a one-way valve for moisture vapor to migrate out of the logs while stopping water from passing through the finish and back into the logs.

There are many different brands of finish on the market today. Most producers of log home finishes typically offer both oil-based and water-based products. As EPA (Environmental Protection Agency) guidelines become more strict, water-based products will continue to be developed and enhanced to minimize the amount of flammable solvents within the finishes. This helps to reduce environmental impact and provides safer handling during both storage and shipment of the products.

In the past, water-based finishes were looked down upon as not being as

durable as the time tested oil-based varieties. However, with increased technology, water-based finishes have proved to be of equal or greater quality. Today, water-based log finishes provide excellent wood preserving properties in a range of beautiful colors while only containing a minimal amount of flammable chemicals.

It is important to note that though great advances have been achieved in water-based finish technology, there is still not a water-based log home finish on the market today that can be applied over a previous oil-based product. If you have a previous finish on your house that you need to recoat and you do not know whether it was oil-based or water-based, it is always best to play it safe and apply an oil-based finish because you can apply oil over water, but you can't apply water over oil.

The 3 Categories

Regardless of the chemical formulation, finishes fit into three basic categories: penetrating, surface coating, or a combination of the two.

Penetrating Finishes

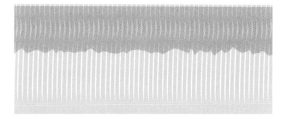

These are historically the oil-based stains that are able to penetrate deep within the wood pores. The advantage of these finishes is that the wood fibers are sealed many cells deep and the pigment is also deeply ingrained.

The downside is that because the finish penetrates the wood surface so deeply, there is little finish left on the surface to repel water and protect the surface layer of the wood from UV rays and surface abrasions. Without a protective surface, the penetrating finish would leach out of the wood through natural weathering.

Another downside to this type of finish is that it takes a larger quantity of finish to adequately cover the house, because of the need to apply numerous coats to build up a protective surface coating.

Surface Film Finishes

This type of finish does not penetrate very deeply into the wood fiber because of the increased particle size of the solids used in the finish. Paint is an obvious example of this type of finish.

Surface film finishes provide excellent water repellency at the cost of being highly susceptible to breakdown from abrasion, though they do protect the wood surface. These are not the type of finishes to be used on logs, steps, decks, or any other high traffic areas.

There is another problem with this type of coating: With a heavy coating on the surface, the wood can not breathe. Any moisture that is trapped beneath the surface of the finished wood will

either quickly rot the wood or blister and crack the surface coating, or both.

Penetrating Film Finishes

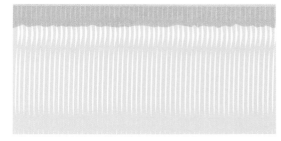

This type is a hybrid of the previous two. Penetrating film finishes attempt to provide the best of both worlds, providing a protecting surface layer film as well as acceptable levels of penetration into the wood fibers.

Most log home finish manufacturers produce finishes that fit roughly into this category. Some provide more of a surface coating whereas others provide more penetration into the wood surface. This "best of both worlds" type of finish is obtained either through a one-part finish in which a single finish formulation is responsible for penetration and surface coating protection, or a two-part finish.

Two-part finishes typically involve one to two coats of a pigmented finish, applied first, and then either one or two coats of a second clear sealing finish that contains fungicides and UV inhibitors. The advantage of these two-part finish systems is that the penetration is handled by one specifically formulated finish, while the surface protection is handled by another. When the clear sealing coat wears down, it is very easy to just clean the surface and then recoat with the clear top coat. The pigmented coat is never touched or affected by the weather.

Considerations When Purchasing a Finish

1. Are your logs green or are they dry (19 percent moisture content or less)?

2. Does your house have long eaves, or lots of trees protecting the walls from the sun?

3. Is your house sitting out in the open with the sun beating down on it all day?

4. Is a high amount of humidity present in your area?

These are questions that should be considered when purchasing a finish for your log house. All finishes are not of the same quality and there is probably one best suited for your conditions that will last at least three to five years. The old adage "You get what you pay for" definitely applies to log home finishes. So you shouldn't expect the bargain basement log oil to last very long.

When purchasing a log home, most owners are aware that there will be some maintenance, but having to redo a finish every one to two years is not something anybody wants to have to do. Look for finishes that are formulated for log homes. Try to find a log house in your area that has the finish you are looking for, so you can see it in use.

Beware of the 7- to 10-year warranties offered by some companies. Read the fine print on how many coats of finish you need to apply to get the 7- to 10-year life out of a finish. Does the finish penetrate into the wood or lay on the surface, making it susceptible to peeling and cracking?

If your logs are green (over 19 percent moisture content) be aware that there are log finishes on the market that are designed for high moisture logs, including the finishes made by Sansin and X-100 Woodcare to name a few. Another option is to let the logs dry for a year before applying a finish.

Remember that wood was a living organism and its cells react not much differently than human skin does. The finish should "breathe" to prevent a buildup of moisture under the finish. Also, the surface needs to be protected; just as sunscreens with higher levels of UV inhibitors protect your skin better, quality finishes protect logs better.

Also consider the cleanup, once you are finished staining your home. Finishes that clean up with soap and water are a lot easier and environmentally safer to handle and dispose of than their oil-based counterparts. Oil-based finishes are typically more toxic, take longer to dry, and produce hazardous fumes. It is important to be aware of these different properties and of what you feel comfortable handling if you are applying the finish yourself.

How Much Log Finish Do I Need?

Length   Width
Perimeter = Length + Width x 2

First, Figure the Walls

1. Measure the outside perimeter of your house. (The perimeter is the distance around your house.) For a four-sided house like the one shown, the perimeter is the Length + the Width x two =_____feet.

2. Multiply the perimeter by the height of your wall. Perimeter x Height = _____sq. ft.

Note: If your house has more than four sides, just take the Wall Length x Wall Height x the Number of Walls = _____sq. ft.

Note: For log walls, add 2 feet to the height of your walls. (This allows for the curvature of the logs.) If you have half-log siding on your house, add only 1 foot to the height. Example: An 8-foot wall made of logs would have an adjusted height of 10 feet.

Next, the Gable Ends

3. To figure the gable ends quickly, multiply the width of the gable by the height of the gable. This will give you the total square footage for both of the gables on your house (if you have only two gables).

Gable Ends =_____sq. ft.

Add It All Up

Now, just add the totals from line 2 and line 3. Total =_____sq. ft.

This area is for the exterior and if you want the total for both exterior and interior, you will need to take this times two. To calculate the total interior amount, you will also need to add for the ceiling and individual interior wall areas and other surfaces.

Windows and Doors?

The question always comes up: What about the area in the windows and doors? These areas could be deducted and then added in for corners, eaves and other areas, or just assume that this will take care of the other areas. If you have wider and longer eaves, you will need to add in or round up the amount of stain needed.

Note: With the square footage in hand, you can calculate the total amount of stain needed by dividing the area by the number of square feet per gallon that the specific stain, finish, or coating will cover. These rates will vary depending on the moisture content, wood species, and the surface quality of the wood (rough or smooth). It is best to factor the lower square footage rate of stain for new construction and the higher rate if there was a previous stain or finish applied.

Finishing and Sealing a New Log Home

This is a brief overview of the steps needed to properly finish and caulk a new log home. Expanded information on these steps can be found in the refinishing section on the next page.

Cleaning: Lightly sandblast, cob blast, sand, or power wash the new logs. When power washing, we suggest you use one of these three types of cleaning agents:

Peroxide Bleach such as CPR works if you will be applying either a water-based or oil-based stain or finish.

Bleach & Water A mixture of 1 part household bleach and 5 parts water, plus 1 tablespoon per gallon TSP (trisodium phosphate) cleaner (optional) per gallon of bleach and water mixture. This works if you will be applying either a water-based or oil-based stain or finish.

Oxalic Acid like X-180 works well as a cleaning agent, especially for sap, pitch, and grease stains.

Apply the cleaning agents from the ground and work up. This will avoid streaking of the logs. Allow to stand for 10–15 minutes before power washing. *Rinse Thoroughly!*

Allow to dry 3–7 days, depending on drying conditions before applying stain (moisture trapped beneath a stain or finish can cause adhesion problems).

Preservative: Apply a borate wood preservative. Depending on the type, some wood preservatives can be applied when the surface is damp. Oil preservatives require dry wood for proper application.

Finish: A pigmented coat of water repellent stain will last longer than a clear finish. Apply one coat (two coats can be applied if moisture content is less than 19 percent) in the first year. Apply a second coat in year 2 only if in year 1 the moisture content is not below 19 percent.

Caulk: On dry wood (19 percent or lower moisture content), caulk in year 1.

On green wood (20 percent or higher moisture content), caulk in year 2.

This allows for more drying of the log joints, to guarantee that the caulking is not overstressed by small caulk joints and large amounts of shrinkage.

Refinishing and Sealing a Log Home

Many people are confused about the proper method when recoating log buildings, so the following may be used as a guide to understanding the process.

1. Surface Preparation

When you are ready to start the refinishing process, begin cleaning the log surfaces by choosing one of the following two methods:

Power Washing This method is very effective and can be used during the drying season (where exterior temperatures are between 65 and 85 degrees, with relative humidity at a level where the wood dries within three to seven days). When spring and fall temperatures are low, in the 30–40s, drying time is lengthened because of the lesser number of hours of adequate drying temperatures.

First, soften the finish coat by spraying on a cleaning agent such as: 1 part household bleach to 5 parts water with an addition of 1 tablespoon of trisodium phosphate (TSP) per gallon of mixture. Other oxidizers such as oxalic acid–based products or peroxide types of bleaches can also be used where there are restrictions on phosphates.

Once the cleaning agent is applied, wait 10 to 30 minutes to use the power washer. The cooler the temperature the longer the wait time, because the chemicals are temperature dependent. Allow the wood to dry until the surface has dried to 19 percent moisture content or less—use a moisture meter to monitor.

Drying time can be three to 10 days depending on the temperatures and

⇨ Inspect Logs for Damage:

Air & Water Infiltration	Signs of Rot	Insects & Other Pests	Caulking or Chinking Problems	Settling Problems: If House is 1–5 Years old *or* If House is 1–10 years old with 16"–18" Logs

⇨ Repair Log Damage:

Caulk Checks	Repair Caulking or Chinking	Install Borate Rods?	Wood Epoxies?	Repair or Replace Logs?	Treat Insects & Pest Damage

⇨ Preventive Maintenance:

Shorten Log Ends or Extend Eaves	Install or Repair Gutters	Landscape to improve run-off drainage	Install Borate Rods?	Apply borate wood preservative after media blasting or chemical stripping?

⇨ Prepare Log Surfaces:

Media Blast or	Chemically Strip or	Sand or	Clean Logs	

⇨ Clean Logs:

Household Bleach & Water	TSP (Optional)	Power Washing	Final Sanding?	

⇨ Caulk or Chink Logs:

Backer Rod Overview	Figure the Amount Needed	Application Steps	Cleanup & Disposal	

⇨ Refinish Logs:

Choose a Finish	Figure the Amount Needed	Apply Finish	Cleanup & Disposal	

An overview of steps and considerations for refinishing a log home.

humidity. When power washing, use 1,250 or less psi to prevent damage to the wood. Read more about power washing on pages 94–95.

Sand- or Cob Blasting

This method can be used at any time because it does not introduce moisture into the system. Because the wood is dry, recoating can take place immediately (once any dust or debris is removed from the logs). This method can change the character of the wood by removing the hard protective shell of the wood and by making the surface rough and more porous.

This method can be used when there is a need to remove heavy coatings or when the temperature and drying conditions are restricting recoating of the log surface.

Depending on the experience of the personnel doing the work, the surface may need to be sanded with a smaller grit sandpaper. This makes the surface more even and closes the wood pores which will reduce the chance of the stain looking blotchy.

The amount of pressure used is dependent on the type of wood and the finish being removed; consult equipment manufactures' recommendations. Read more about sand, cob and other media blasting on pages 96–97.

2. Prime the Worn or Weathered Area

Once the surface is dried, there may be areas where the finish was removed by the cleaning process. It is now time to apply a finish to these areas to bring the color to the same level as the surrounding areas. This priming may require a diluted coat of stain or one or more full pigment coats. The objective is to bring the areas as close to the color and texture of the surrounding surfaces as possible.

3. Caulking and Wood Replacement

If corners or other areas need caulking or if wood replacement is required, take care of those requirements at this time. Again, if there is wood replacement done, prime those areas as discussed in item 2.

During the process of caulking, remember that upward facing cracks in the wood that are 3⁄16 inch wide or larger can collect and hold moisture. This is also true of flat shelf-like areas. When the areas hold moisture, the heat of the sun pulls the moisture into the wood, under the stain, and forces the finish off the wood surface. By paying attention to these problem areas you can prevent rot and underperformance of the finish.

It is recommended, if a compatible finish is used, to apply one coat of finish first and then caulk and apply another coat of finish. A compatible finish is one that does not prevent adhesion because of large amounts of waxes or other ingredients that may affect adhesion. Most finishes are not a problem but paraffinic oils can be. When in doubt do a 21-day peel test: Apply a strip of caulking to a stained surface, wait 21 days, and then check to see if caulk pulls off the stained surface. This is the process used in testing labs to determine adhesion qualities.

Note: On new construction of handcrafted buildings where large green logs are used, it is recommended to apply one coat of stain, wait one year, apply the caulk and then apply the second coat of stain. This process is also recommended with the three-coat stains on the market. If you are recoating these types of buildings early on, moisture may have been the problem. Moisture can cause rot and also reduce adhesion to the surface.

4. Start the Recoating Process

Which is best, spraying or brushing? The main consideration is an even continuous coating of the finish. Either method can be used, but brushing may force the stain into the wood better.

Spraying can be used along with back-brushing to obtain an even film. In the spraying process there may be more likelihood of areas where a thinner coating is applied, and these areas weather out earlier. Another risk is that the introduction of air may cause the finish to dry too fast and keep it from absorbing into the wood to create better adhesion to the surface.

Also, be aware that the top surface of the log is affected by the weathering process more than the lower half of the log, and this area needs more attention in the recoating process. During this process also be aware that each layer of finish has wearing qualities dependent on the thickness of the film. So, more coats will usually give more life and the type of the finish can cause varying coat thicknesses.

In the past it was usually thought that water-based finishes required more coats to reach the same film thickness as an oil-based finish. Today many of the water-based finishes have qualities similar to the oil finishes of the past.

Another common question is this: Are darker stains or finishes better than lighter colored stains or finishes? The color is more important at the beginning stages, during log curing. Lighter colors will help reflect heat and because of this the logs may dry more slowly and not check or crack as much on the surface.

Later in the life of the building, darker stains may be selected, not because they are better but because weathered gray areas are not noticed as readily; thus people looking at your home may believe that the finish is lasting longer because the weathered areas are not as noticeable.

The main elements enabling a stain to perform to its maximum are the amount of solids, the amount of mildewcides, and the flexibility to extreme weathering which is determined by the amount of light exposure (sun) and the amount of ultraviolet light blockers. Most of these are limited by what can be added to the finish and yet to be effective without being cost prohibitive. In areas of excessive moisture or insect activity, these additives are often used to boost performance.

Power Washing Logs

Power Wash Exterior Logs Only

The interior surfaces are not critical, since they are not exposed to extreme weather.

Power Wash New Logs

To remove any leftover mill glaze and lightly roughen the surface to allow stain to penetrate as deeply as possible. (Mill glaze is the stain-repelling film left over from shaping the logs in the processing mill.)

Power Wash Pre-finished Logs

To remove dirt, spiderwebs, or flaking or peeling stain, and lightly roughen the surface to allow the stain to penetrate as deeply as possible.

Step 1.
Use Bleach & Water to Clean

Apply a mixture of 1 part household bleach to 5 parts water on the lower logs and work your way upwards to avoid streaking the logs. On heavily weathered logs, you may need to use a 1:3 mixture. Use a more diluted mixture on softer, more porous woods like cedar.

TSP (trisodium phosphate) cleaner can be added (1 tablespoon to the bleach and water) to increase cleaning effectiveness. If you choose to use TSP as a cleaner and use it in heavy amounts, it can pull out the reddish undertones in red pine (Norway pine). This red undertone can react with yellow finishes to give an orange appearance to the logs. Bleach and TSP can harm vegetation, so be sure to cover flowerbeds and shrubbery with plastic or waterproof tarps to minimize exposure.

Step 2.
Let Bleach & Water Set 10–15 Minutes

impact the wood with tremendous force and will remove virtually all residues, as well as creating considerable micro-roughening of the surface for enhanced stain adhesion.

Note: If your logs become "fuzzy" or "hairy," this condition will not affect the performance of the stain, but it can be objectionable in appearance. Sanding and polishing the logs with an Osborn buffing brush afterwards can minimize the fuzzy appearance.

Chlorine bleach is **NOT** environmentally friendly and can be destructive to the wood if it remains on the logs too long. Rinse thoroughly!

Alternatives to Bleach & Water
Other alternatives to bleach and water include oxalic acids like X-180 and peroxide bleaches like CPR, but regular household bleach and water is the most common and readily available.

Avoid Soaking the Interior
Before power washing, check the condition of the chinking and caulking for cracks or separations. Caulk and chinking problems will need to be repaired before power washing (see *Caulking & Chinking Problem Solving* starting on page 64). If not repaired, water will be forced deep into the log joints, exposing the wood to possible rot and insect infestation as well as volumes of water flooding the inside of your home.

Avoid Breaking Windows
Do not spray directly at windows with a power washer; this could cause breakage and the flooding of the inside of your house with water.

Step 3.
Power Wash from the Top Down
Use a fan spray nozzle at 1500 psi or lower at an angle so it does not spray back into your face. Be sure to wear safety goggles or other eye protection. Power washing should be done with as little pressure as necessary to remove dirt and debris without physically damaging the log surfaces. Start with a low pressure and adjust it gradually upwards to minimize damage or excessive fuzzing to the wood.

Hold the nozzle at a distance, just far enough away from the surface to avoid "fuzzing" the outer layer of wood. This will take a little practice to get the feel of it. At this distance, the spray will

Sandblasting Logs

Silicosis is permanent lung damage that can cause shortness of breath and increased risk of tuberculosis (TB), and can be fatal.

If you decide to have your logs sandblasted be sure to have the work done by a seasoned professional who has had experience with logwork. A sandblasting novice can do severe, irreparable damage to the logs. Extreme pressure can cut unsightly gouges into logs and other woodwork. Unprotected windows can be pitted with an etched appearance. Sandblasting log homes is generally best left to a log home restoration professional.

Sandblasting is an effective way of stripping logs of previous finishes. Sandblasting utilizes silica sand as an abrasive element to pneumatically grind away the old finish. Once the logs have been sandblasted, they will need to be sanded down to minimize the light pitting that occurs. The amount of pitting that can occur is dependent on the type of wood being sandblasted and the amount of blasting pressure used.

Protective equipment is necessary when sandblasting is performed. A serious health condition called silicosis can develop in sandblaster operators if protective equipment is not used properly.

A Sandblasting Alternative: Glass

Recycled crushed glass has been used as a successful alternative to sand as a blasting material. The crushed glass looks similar to sand, but it is chemically inert and the dust will not cause silicosis.

The crushed glass has been found to be less expensive than sand and it does an excellent job of removing previous finishes from logs and woodwork.

Cob Blasting Logs

Cob blasting is the newest environmentally friendly way of stripping logs by using dried corn cobs, instead of sand. Cob blasting won't pit the logs the way that sandblasting will and is also less abrasive than using sand.

Once used, the cob media can be used as mulch for a garden or around plants when the job is done (if the stripped finish doesn't contain any lead). Typically with sandblasting the sand has to be hauled away, adding an extra expense to the overall project.

Critics of cob blasting claim that the cob media is an excellent material for transporting fungus into the logs. The concern is that the fungus is already in infected bags of media or just as simply fertile ground for fungus to grow in. If the logs are treated with a borate wood preservative after cob blasting, the issue becomes moot.

A light sanding of the logs is all that is required after cob blasting so that absorption of stain is more uniform and so you can save time and expense by not having to sand the logs down so heavily.

Cob blasting is most often a service of professional log home chinking and finish applicators. Generally, most homeowners prefer not to do the work themselves and leave the work to a log home restoration professional.

Soda Blasting Logs

Soda (sodium bicarbonate) blasting was developed in the 1970s as a more environmentally friendly, non-toxic alternative to sandblasting, for restoration of the Statue of Liberty. Soda blasting is not as abrasive as sandblasting and does far less damage to the surface. This aspect saves on extra sanding labor once the blasting has been finished.

An example of charred logs that were cleaned and deodorized by soda blasting.

Like its food-grade counterpart—baking soda—sodium bicarbonate does a great job of absorbing odors and so is highly recommended for smoke and fire damage restoration. Wall logs that have been charred black can quickly and easily be restored so that no one would ever know that they had been fire damaged.

Sodium bicarbonate has a pH of 8.4 and can raise the alkalinity of nearby soil and have a detrimental effect on vegetation. This can be overcome by spraying down plants and shrubbery with water before and after soda blasting. Sodium bicarbonate can also break down hydrocarbons and so care should be taken to protect asphalt surfaces near the blasting area.

To help you find a company that provides soda blasting services, you can contact **Disaster Kleenup International**:

USA Head Office
7301 Georgetown Rd., Suite 108
Indianapolis, IN 46268
Phone: 317-334-7600
Toll Free: 1-800-567-8047
Fax: 317-334-7610

Canadian Head Office
5770 Timberlea Blvd., Suite 203
Mississauga, ON L4W 4W7
Phone: 905-238-6288
Toll Free: 1-800-461-6224
Fax: 905-238-6411

www.disasterkleenup.com

Chemical Strippers

Another effective, but potentially highly caustic, way of stripping logs of previous finishes is chemical strippers. Chemical strippers can pose serious health risks to the user if misused or used carelessly. They also pose possible environmental hazards, especially if the work is being done near open bodies of water. The most caustic type of strippers contains methylene chloride (also known as dichloromethane—DCM) and can be flammable as well as carcinogenic. Other caustic and/or flammable ingredients that can be found in these types of strippers include acetone, toluene, and methanol.

There are a number of chemical strippers on the market that are more environmentally friendly and less hazardous to use. Such examples include Peelaway, CitriStrip, and Super Bio Strip. These products can remove both latex and oil-based paints and finishes and can be either scraped off the wood surfaces or washed away with a garden hose providing that the removed finish does not contain lead.

These types of strippers are recommended if you need to strip interior logs or woodwork. Though these strippers are not as caustic as those containing methylene chloride, protective equipment including eye and hand protection should be used. An approved air mask should be worn when using chemical strippers inside the house; be sure to have adequate ventilation including fans to push vapors out and away from the house.

Be sure to read and follow all warnings and directions for the product that you are using. Check with your local sanitation department for local regulations for disposal of stripped paint and finish material. Because of the potential safety, health, and environmental hazards, many homeowners prefer to hire a professional to do the stripping and disposal work.

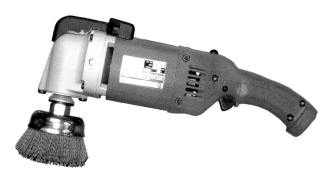

Sanding Your Logs

Both cob and sandblasting will pit the logs to varying degrees depending on the wood species (the softer the wood, the more chance of deeper pitting) and the skill of the operator. After cob blasting, sandblasting, or power washing, the log surface usually needs some degree of sanding to smooth the surface appearance. Sanding not only gives the logs a smooth, uniform surface but also opens up the wood pores, which helps the finish to soak deep into the wood grain.

The most practical method is to use a nylon bristled, 80 grit, 6-inch or 8-inch buffing brush attached to an angle grinder (shown above) or car buffer. One of the best brushes in the log home market is the Osborn buffing brush. It usually takes two brushes at low rpm speeds to do an average-sized log house. Otherwise, orbital hand sanders are a good alternative.

Log Home Finish Problem Solving

Logs Were Never Finished

For whatever reason, the logs seen here were never finished and now show signs of rot and decay. Entire logs may need to be replaced, depending on the length of time the logs have been in this condition.

Treatment
The logs will need to be thoroughly inspected for advanced stages of rot. Logs that are soft and "punky" may need replacement. If a 4-inch nail can easily be pushed into the log, it may need either half-log or full log replacement. If in doubt, contact a log restoration contractor. They will be able to professionally inspect, make recommendations, and perform restoration services.

If logs are not rotted too severely, impel rods can be installed to minimize future damage. See *Impel Rods* on pages 138–139.

It may be that the logs just need sand-blasting, cob blasting, or power washing with 1 part bleach and 5 parts water to remove the mold, mildew, and gray appearance. A tablespoon of TSP can also be added to the bleach and water mixture to provide extra cleaning action. Read more about power washing on pages 94–95.

Make sure that the logs are rinsed well with clear water and allow the log surfaces to dry completely. Coat the logs with a quality log home finish, following the manufacturer's directions.

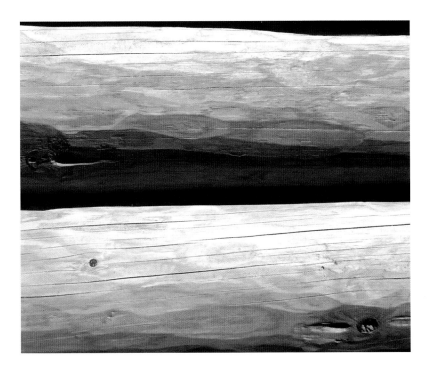

Log Home Finish Needs Recoating

Here, the log finish looks okay; there are no visual signs of peeling or cracking, discoloration, mold, or mildew. Overall, the finish looks the way the home-owner intended it to look.

However, what you don't see is that if you splash a little water on the finish, the water fails to bead up and roll off; instead, it just fans out and soaks into the finish and wood. The finish on this log home is three or four years old and has totally lost its water repellency.

Now is the perfect time to recoat, *before* the logs begin to discolor, chip, fade, or attract mold and mildew. By renewing the finish with a maintenance coat at this stage you will save both time and money, whether you do the work yourself or pay a professional to do the work for you. Log surfaces will need minimal cleanup and preparation before recoating. And because you only need to add one maintenance coat, you will save on the costs of stripping the logs plus refinishing with two or three coats of finish.

Treatment

In most cases like this, the logs could just be rinsed down with a garden hose and then allowed to thoroughly dry before recoating. If the rinsing fails to remove all dirt and debris, the logs can be lightly power washed to clean them of all pollen, dust, and debris. Allow the log surfaces to dry completely and then recoat with finish following the manufacturer's guidelines.

Lap Marks in Finish

You can see the definite streak in the finish where one side is lighter than the other side. This happened when the logs were being finished. The applicator stopped at that point (probably at the end of the day) and then resumed later (probably the next morning). The overlap area of the finish will always cause a dark streak in the wall because of the buildup of finish in that particular area.

Prevention
When coating logs with stain or finish, never stop in the middle of a wall. Finish the entire wall before taking a break or quitting for the day. Coating across an entire log is also a good way to prevent lap marks.

Treatment
Other than stripping off the finish, you could go back and try to touch up the area, feathering from darker to lighter. This blending may not completely remove the lap mark but will make it less noticeable.

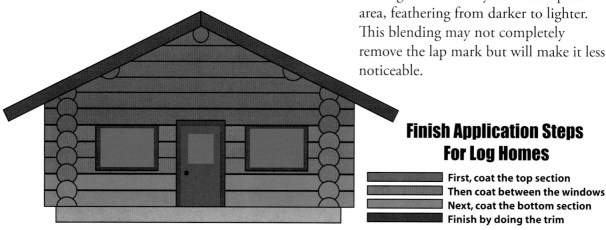

Finish Application Steps For Log Homes

First, coat the top section
Then coat between the windows
Next, coat the bottom section
Finish by doing the trim

By following these commonly accepted steps for finish application, you can minimize the possibility of streaking. Remember to always finish an entire log before stopping.

Cambium & Inner Bark Left on the Logs

The dark streaks on the closeup of this log are portions of the inner bark that were left on the log when the log was drawknifed. Beneath the inner bark is the cambium layer. Cambium is a soft wood membrane that lies between the bark and the sapwood of the log.

It is important to note that if you do have inner bark and cambium left on the logs, finishes and inner bark will tend to peel away from the cambium beneath it. Most people will think that it was because the finish was defective, but really what happens is that the cambium pulls away from the sapwood beneath it and forces the finish to peel with it. This problem is more common on the exterior finishes than on the interior.

Treatment

If peeling has started, it will only become worse with age. If the cambium is on the exterior of the house, remove the finish and cambium by media blasting with cob, sand, soda, etc. If the cambium is on the interior of the house, media blasting becomes a very messy prospect.

Sanding the finish off with orbital sanders is labor intensive, though a less messy alternative. A wet-dry vac can be operated by one person, catching the dust and debris while another sands the logs. Make sure that all sanding dust has been removed from the logs before recoating with finish.

If the logs were never treated with a borate wood preservative, one should be applied, primarily to the exterior logs, once the finish, inner bark, and cambium have been removed. After the logs have thoroughly dried from the preservative treatment, recoat with a quality log home finish.

Thick Finish Coating
Chipped & Peeling

This is a serious condition and should be attended to as soon as possible to minimize future damage from rot and insect infestation. The thick, heavy buildup of paint or finish coating will eventually break down and start to chip and peel. Usually this is caused by expansion and contraction of the logs, which pull away from the hard shell surface coating.

Peeling can also result from a water-based finish erroneously applied over an oil-based finish. A water-based finish will pull away from the oil-based finish beneath it. However, oil-based finishes can be applied over water-based finishes. As log home finish technology evolves, this may change in future formulations.

Treatment
Remove the finish by media blasting with cob, sand, soda, etc. If the cambium is on the interior of the house, media blasting becomes a very messy prospect.

Sanding the finish off with orbital sanders is labor intensive, though a less messy alternative. A wet-dry vac can be operated by one person, catching the dust and debris while another sands the logs. Make sure that all sanding dust has been removed from the logs before recoating with finish.

If the logs were never treated with a borate wood preservative, one should be applied, primarily to the exterior logs, once the finish and cambium have been removed.

After the logs have thoroughly dried from the preservative treatment, recoat with a quality log home finish.

Painted Logs with Signs of Rot

This example shows an extreme situation where the paint coating has cracked and water has entered the wood through the cracks, starting to rot it. The paint coating has acted like a plastic wrap that has kept water in the logs, accelerating the decay process. Algae have started to grow on the paint surface because of the wet environment. The log has become so soft from rot that you can push your finger down into the log with little resistance.

Prevention

Paint should never be used on logs. Log home finishes are specially formulated to adhere and protect logs by providing water repellency while allowing the logs to "breathe."

Yearly monitoring of the condition of the logwork, finish, and chinking of your log structures will minimize the possibility of a situation like this getting out of hand.

Treatment

With the log being so rotted, the log or logs may need to be replaced. Depending on the situation, half-log replacement might be a much more affordable option. Keep in mind that there may be much more damage beneath the viewable surface in many different areas of the log building.

In a situation like this, you may be just scratching the surface of a much larger restoration project. Severely rotted logs or timbers have the potential of causing endangerment due to loss of structural stability.

Consult with a number of log home restoration contractors and obtain bids for doing the log repair and an overall assessment of the structure. If you are interested in doing the work yourself see *Log Restoration* on pages 134–165.

Mold Growing on Logs

Using a linseed oil–based finish that does not contain adequate mildewcides can cause mold to grow on logs. Mold will actually feed on linseed oil and then on the wood. This condition can also be caused by applying a finish when the logs are heavily shaded, constantly damp, or moist from dew or high humidity. Another cause is the finish wearing down naturally without maintenance coats. Bare wood is exposed, making it easy for mold and mildew to infest.

Treatment

If the mold is growing underneath the finish, remove the finish by media blasting with cob, sand, soda, etc., or by using a chemical stripper. See pages 96–99. Lighten mold stains with a wash of 1 part household bleach and 4–5 parts water or with X-180. Rinse off the bleach or other cleaner thoroughly. A borate preservative like PeneTreat can be applied to the bare wood to help protect against future mold and mildew (follow manufacturer's directions and precautions). Allow the logs to completely dry and then refinish.

If the mold is growing on the surface of the logs, power wash lightly with household bleach and water. Rinse thoroughly; allow the logs to thoroughly dry, and then recoat with a finish that doesn't contain only linseed oil.

Mold and Mildew Growing behind the Finish

This is a serious situation and needs to be dealt with immediately. The logs were too green when a water repellent coating was applied. Moisture became locked inside the logs. It then became the perfect environment for mold and mildew to grow. The black areas are mold and the white area near the top of the picture is mildew. The fungi grew soon after the logs were finished and quickly went to work rotting the logs.

Treatment

Remove the coating by either sanding or grinding the finish away with orbital sanders or using a chemical stripper. If using a stripper, read all the directions and take proper precautions.

Once the finish is removed, allow the logs to dry out. An air conditioner in the house can help to pull moisture out of the logs, but you have to be careful not to let them dry out too fast or huge cracks or checks can open up in the logs. Use window fans to push the moisture out of the house.

The dark mold stains will never come completely out of the logs. Washing them using a mixture of 1 part bleach to 4–5 parts water can lighten them. You can also try an oxalic acid like X-180. Rinse thoroughly and allow the logs to dry completely. Once the logs have dried out (use a moisture meter to make sure the logs are 19 percent or less moisture content) apply a new finish.

Sunburned Logs with Semi-Transparent Stain

You can see the dark patches on the top part of the logs, caused by the sun's ultraviolet rays penetrating through the finish and sunburning the logs. This happens as the log finish ages and the UV inhibitors within the finish start to breakdown. UV inhibitor break down will actually be accelerated by large amounts of direct sunlight reflected on the finish.

Treatment

Media blast the logs with cob, sand, glass, etc. to remove the finish and sunburned areas. Make sure all of the blasting and/or sanding residue is removed before recoating with a quality log home finish.

You could use a buffing brush or orbital sander to sand down the sunburned areas and then either recoat the logs or touch up the areas with finish.

However, keep in mind that the sanded wood will absorb the finish at a greater rate than the unsanded areas of wood, giving the finish a noticeably uneven or blotchy look. Many times a thinned-out first coat may need to be applied as a primer coat to reduce the heavy absorption of a pigmented finish.

Another sunburning example on half-log siding. The wood surface will become darker as the amount of sunburning increases.

Sunburning and Peeling of a Clear Finish

Clear finishes contain little if any UV inhibitors and quickly break down from direct sunlight within six months to a year. The condition is always more severe on the southern or sunny sides of the log home. Also, small microchecking can allow moisture to enter wood and then come in under the finish to loosen it. You can see where the log has been exposed to the sun on top and has sunburned and turned gray. The finish is also peeling and needs to be redone.

Prevention
Clear finishes should not be used on the exterior of log homes. Semi-transparent log home stains are a far better alternative. A yearly inspection of the finish will minimize the chance of a finish deteriorating so severely.

Treatment
Remove the finish by media blasting using cob or sand, or soda. Once the finish has been completely removed, a borate wood preservative like PeneTreat is recommended. The wood preservative can only be applied to bare wood and this is an excellent time to apply (if not previously applied when the house was new). Wait for the preservative to completely dry before refinishing.

Refinish using a quality semi-transparent log home finish to provide longer lasting protection while maintaining a coating that enhances the wood grain. Be sure to follow the manufacturer's guidelines.

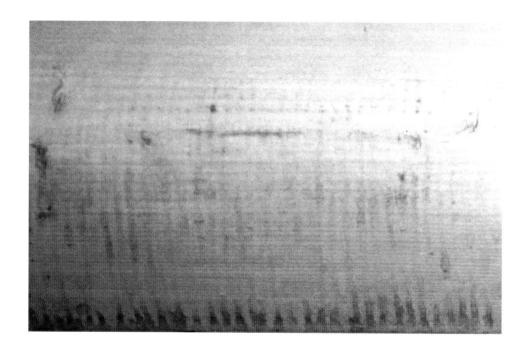

"Coffee Staining" on Logs

The discolored drip marks found on these logs are referred to as "coffee staining." The term comes from the wood appearing as though coffee has been spilled on it. In actuality, the staining is caused by bleach solutions or other cleaning agents that were not completely rinsed off or by mildewcides or sapstain control products that did not thoroughly coat the entire surface of the logs. When the wood is finished, the stains usually become more noticeable, causing a contrast of light and dark.

Coffee staining is a visual annoyance more than anything else and does not mean that the wood is damaged or more prone to rot or insect infestation then non-coffee-stained wood. If the staining is caused by bleach not being thoroughly rinsed off, the bleach can be destructive to finishes.

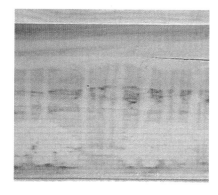

Prevention
When applying sapstain controls, make sure that the entire log is equally coated. When washing logs with bleach or other cleaning agents, make sure that the wood is fully rinsed.

Treatment
Remove the finish and sand the wood with an Osborn buffing brush or orbital sanders to remove stains. The stains may not be completely removed, but can be lightened by this method. Recoat with finish. If the staining does not lighten, it may be brown stain.

Brown Stain on Logs

Brown stain can be caused by sapstain fungi or from chemical stains (enzymatic oxidation) that appear as the wood dries. The fungi attack trees before they are cut or just after they are cut. Unlike coffee staining, brown stain and other sapstain cannot be removed or lightened from the wood. Sapstain does not structurally alter the strength of wood, but it can cause wood to absorb moisture more easily.

Prevention

A sapstain control like LogKeeper, TM-5 First Treat, or Timber-Tec applied to the logs after they have been cut and peeled will greatly minimize sapstain discoloration. Chemical stains are promoted by slow drying in warm or hot temperatures and can be avoided by kiln drying wood at low temperatures.

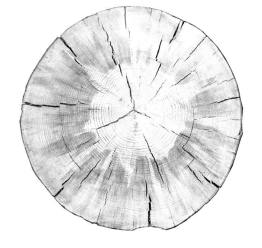

An end cut view showing blue stain in a log that has not been treated with a sapstain control.

Treatment

If you find the brown stain or other sapstain discolorations objectionable, all you can do is use a darker color finish to make the stains less noticeable, or discard the affected wood.

Finish Worn Away from Logs

This is a severe case of the log finish being worn away. The logs may have been too damp when finished or the temperature may have been too cold for the proper application and adhesion of the finish. Another possibility is that the logs were not properly sanded before the finish was applied. Other causes aside from failure to recoat with finish in a timely manner include the logs being dusty or dirty, or coated with some other residue prior to finishing. These situations will cause adhesion problems for the finish and promote premature degradation.

Treatment

The logs can be lightly power washed to remove the remaining finish. Allow the logs to dry, then sand and polish them with an Osborn buffing brush to remove any fuzzing. Rinse the logs to remove any fine sawdust left by the buffing brush and allow to dry completely.

With the finish removed, a borate wood preservative like PeneTreat could be applied to give additional protection to the wood from future rot and insect infestation (if it was not applied during construction).

When the wood has dried from the borate application, refinish with a quality log home stain or finish. Be sure to follow the manufacturer's directions and guidelines.

Backsplash Problems #1

In this situation, the lack of rain gutters allowed rainwater to drip down and backsplash against the bottom logs. If not taken care of, the gray discoloration of the lower logs will turn to rot and eventually cause structural damage to the building. Insects will also be attracted to the wet, decaying wood and will start to infest.

Treatment

First, power wash the walls to remove the remaining finish. Use a plastic scrub brush and a mixture of 1 part bleach and 5 parts water plus 1 tablespoon of trisodium phosphate to clean the grayness from the logs. Rinse the logs thoroughly with clean water. Allow the logs to dry and then sand and polish them with an Osborn buffing brush. Rinse the logs to remove any fine sawdust left by the buffing brush and allow to completely dry.

With the finish removed, a borate wood preservative like PeneTreat could be applied to give additional protection to the wood from future rot and insect infestation (if it was not applied during construction). Refinish with a quality log home finish following the manufacturer's directions and guidelines.

Finally, install rain gutters to redirect water away from the log walls to prevent future damage.

Backsplash Problems #2

Here, you can see that flashing was used on the entryway and gutters are in place on both roof edges. Unfortunately, these devices offered little protection to the log wall. This situation can also be caused or exacerbated when snow is piled up on a roof next to an exterior wall. This is a particularly troublesome design issue and will continue to be problematic. The only thing that can be done in a situation like this is to be aware that this is a problem area, and keep up on the maintenance.

Treatment

First, power wash the walls to remove what little finish remains. Use a plastic scrub brush and a mixture of 1 part household bleach and 5 parts water plus 1 tablespoon of trisodium phosphate to clean the grayness from the logs. Rinse the logs thoroughly with clean water. Allow the logs to dry thor-

oughly and then sand and polish them with an Osborn buffing brush. Rinse the logs to remove any fine sawdust left by the buffing brush and allow to dry completely. Refinish or touch up as necessary with a quality log home finish.

Make sure that rain gutters are clean and in good working order. The angle of the gutters can shift as the logs settle, forcing water towards the house instead of away from it. Test the gutters by having someone on the roof pour water into the gutters. Fix any leaks that appear. Replace if necessary. Also make sure that shrubbery near the house is removed to avoid backsplashing hazards.

Periodically check the condition of the chinking of the logs and the caulking around the windows to make sure that water cannot infiltrate the logwork.

Backsplash Problems #3

The lack of rain gutters and entryway has allowed rainwater to backsplash off the stairs and against the lower logs. The gray discoloration of the lower logs will turn to rot and eventually cause structural damage to the building. The firewood stacked next to the building also allows water to backsplash onto the logs, causing similar damage. Insects that have infested the firewood can also easily migrate to the house logs.

Treatment

Media blast the logs with cob, sand, or soda, to remove the finish and gray areas. Sand with an Osborn buffing brush to smooth and polish the logs. Make sure all of the blasting and/or sanding residue is removed before recoating with a quality log home finish.

Check the condition of the logs that were discolored. If a nail can be pushed easily into the wood, the logs will need to be repaired by patching, half-log, or full-log replacement (see *Chapter 9: Log Restoration* on pages 134–165).

Install rain gutters and move the stacks of firewood to a sheltered area away from the house to prevent future damage. Consider building an entryway to protect the stairs and log walls. If you do not wish to build an entryway, it is advisable to install impel rods in the affected logs. See *Impel Rods* on pages 138–139.

Backsplash Problems #4

Sill logs should never have direct contact with ground soil. The end of this sill log has completely deteriorated from backsplashing and lack of regular maintenance. The constant exposure to the elements has caused brown rot and algae to eat through the finish and turn the wood to a soft mush. The northeast corners of log homes can be very problematic when close to the ground; the sun and air movement are usually not sufficient to dry the wood out.

Prevention

The sill logs should be a minimum of 2 feet above ground. Longer roof overhang (2 feet or more) would also minimize the backsplashing effects of rainwater. Regular inspection of the sill logs would have caught the problem before it advanced to this stage of decay. Impel rods can also be used to provide protection from rot and insects.

Treatment

For a condition like this, the log end will have to be cut out and replaced. The new log ends are called log crowns. Read more about log crowns on pages 142–149 for info about this replacement process. Usually, a log restoration contractor is called in to do this type of crown replacement.

Once the new crowns have been installed, impel rods should be used to help protect the new crown against future rot, decay, and insect infestation. Impel rods are highly recommended when sill logs are within 2 feet of the ground and the wood is vulnerable to excessive backsplashing. See *Impel Rods* on pages 138–139.

Finish Worn Away from Log Ends

The finish of this exposed log end has worn away and turned white from bleaching in the sun.

Prevention

The finish on the log ends can be touched up periodically to maintain protection. The log ends could have been profiled to reduce the amount of surface exposure to the sun. Another alternative used in Europe and in earlier times is to simply cover the ends with trim boards.

Treatment

Because most of the finish has worn away, all that is really needed is to make sure the surface is clean and dry before recoating with a quality log home finish.

The endgrain of the logs will act like a sponge, absorbing more finish than the sidegrain of the walls will. You can typically put one or two extra coats on the log ends to fully seal them.

The log ends could be profiled to minimize their exposure to direct sunlight. The concave profile will shade the log ends and give them a custom look while not affecting any structural integrity.

Original Logs (Sideview)

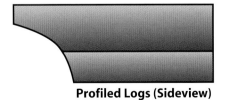

Profiled Logs (Sideview)

Sap Seeping from Sides of Finished Logs

Sap and pitch can seep from logs for years after the logs have been cut and the building finished. This usually happens when a lot of moisture is leaving the wood, carrying pitch to the surface. Also, the logs could have been summer cut when they contained more moisture, sap, and pitch. It is always best to cut logs during the winter months or early spring when moisture, sap, and pitch are at a minimum. The photo above was taken of a house that was four years old.

Treatment
If the sap or pitch is dry and crystallized it can be scraped off with a metal putty knife or sanded off with an Osborn buffing brush; the remaining residue can be cleaned up with a mild solvent such as rubbing alcohol.

If the sap or pitch is still wet, wait until it has stopped running. A cleaning agent like X-180 can be used to remove the wet sap, or let it dry and then clean up with a mild solvent like rubbing alcohol. If you clean it off while it is still wet, it will probably continue to ooze back out over the area you have cleaned. You may want to just let the sap continue to seep out until it stops before trying to clean it up.

> *A single cypress log once produced 50 gallons of sap over an extended period of time.*
>
> *How much sap is in your logs? Only time will tell.*

Sap Seeping from Finished Log Ends

Here is another example from a four-year-old house. Sap and pitch will seep most commonly from the log ends.

Treatment

If the sap or pitch is dry and crystallized it can be scraped off with a metal putty knife. The remaining residue can be cleaned up with a mild solvent such as rubbing alcohol.

If the sap or pitch is still wet, wait until it has stopped running. Let it dry and then clean up with solvent. If you clean it off while it is still wet, it will probably continue to ooze back out over the area you have cleaned.

If you will be refinishing the house, consider using an end sealer such as Sealtite 60 to help seal the log ends. End sealers are wax based products and may affect the adhesive qualities of the log finish that you coat over them, so you may want to apply the end sealer over the cured finish. When it is time to recoat, use a solvent to remove the end sealer and refinish as you normally would.

You can obtain similar end sealing by using a paintbrush to force as much finish into the log end as it will hold. Let the finish dry and then apply an extra coat to the ends, again forcing as much finish as possible into the ends. Log ends are more porous and will absorb more finish than the sides of logs.

Chapter 8: Log Home Decks

Decks probably take more abuse than any other exterior wood surface around your home. They must weather the extremes of full sun exposure, rain, snow, and ice. Standing water and slow-melting snow and ice are problematic for decks because their flat surfaces do not repel water through runoff and so the deck finish has to act as a water barrier. Microfissures such as small checks and cracks in the wood surface allow water to seep in under the finish and help to cause the finish to release or peel.

Decks and deck finishes are also susceptible to high levels of surface abrasion caused by normal wear from foot traffic, deck furniture and barbecue grills being moved around, and snow and ice removal, not to mention the wear and tear of pet claws. Decks must also endure stains from greasy barbe-

cues, as well as spilled beverages and toppled food items.

It is easy to see that the prospect of maintaining a beautiful deck finish year after year has the potential of being a lot of hard work. It is important to consider what your expectations are when it comes to the appearance of your deck finish, and how much you are willing to do in order to meet those expectations.

For those who want their decks to have a glossy or satin "furniture-like" appearance by building up translucent layers of film finish to show the depth of grain, keep in mind that these finishes are the most prone to failure due to blistering, peeling, and abrasion wear. Film forming finishes do provide an excellent water-repelling barrier as long as the film barrier is not broken or penetrated by moisture. The problem is, they do break down through surface abrasion or water penetrating microfissures and checks, making blistering and peeling inevitable.

Other non–film forming finishes that penetrate deeper into the wood and have little surface film will provide a both protective and attractive finish. This type of deck finish will not readily fail due to blistering and peeling.

These coatings have the advantage of looking good for a period of time and then wearing or fading away. Because there is no heavy surface buildup to be physically removed, recoating is much easier and should be done before the deck finish is totally worn away. This is necessary not only to keep the finish looking good but also to ensure that the finish is providing adequate wood protection.

The schedule for recoating of this type of finish is anywhere from one to three years. This timeframe is determined by the amount of physical wear and direct sunlight that the deck receives throughout the year.

The Key Is Wood Preparation

The most important step when finishing a deck is the preparation of the wood prior to coating. This step is often overlooked or hastily performed which results in premature breakdown of the finish and decreased durability, as well as a poor appearance. It is important to read and understand the following material in order to apply the necessary course of action for your particular project. Scientists have found that bare wood exposed to direct sun-

light for one to two weeks or as little as four to five days can photo-chemically alter the wood surface causing premature adhesion failure of practically any finish coating. The reason is that the sun's ultraviolet rays break down the surface wood fiber, and though the finish adheres properly, the surface wood fibers will break away from the wood fibers beneath.

For New Decks

Regardless of the species, new lumber, either pressure treated or not, often contains excessive internal moisture. In order for a finish to properly adhere, the excess moisture needs to be removed. This is done through natural seasoning—just letting the wood dry out naturally. This process can take days or months depending on the amount of moisture contained within the wood and the atmospheric conditions of the region.

Use a moisture meter to monitor the wood's moisture content. A moisture meter is a reliable means for detecting and monitoring moisture levels. For proper adhesion of the majority of deck finishes, the moisture content of the wood should be 19 percent or less. Keep in mind that the wood may register different moisture levels at different areas of the lumber and so it is important to take a number of readings to insure that all of the wood is at the proper moisture content.

If you are in the process of building a deck, it is a good idea to build with dry lumber so the cut ends can be coated with a deck finish prior to assembly. Finishing all six sides of the lumber prior to construction is considered a "best-case scenario." Whether or not you plan on coating all six sides prior to building, make sure that any UV-damaged surface wood and/or mill glaze on the lumber has been removed before applying a deck finish. To keep deck boards from cupping, make sure that the growth rings at the end of the lumber crown upwards. Also, use deck clips as attachments to minimize the amount of holes in the upper face of the lumber.

Mill glaze is the stain-repelling film that is caused from the outer wood cells being condensed during the milling process. Mill glaze can be removed through prolonged exposure of the wood to the elements and is recommended for pressure treated lumber. Natural weathering of wind, sun, and rain will break down the mill-glazed surface in approximately six to 12 months, depending on the local climate. During this time, however, the wood is exposed to fungus, insects, and UV damage; take this into consideration if you plan to follow this method. Your other choice is to remove mill glaze and UV damage by power washing, sanding, or media blasting (cob, sand, glass, or soda).

Power Washing

This is a common method that can easily be done by the homeowner. The real key to proficient power washing is to get the pressure just right so that dirt, debris, and mill glaze are removed without taking off excess wood. When too much of the wood surface is removed, a "fuzzy" or "hairy" appearance develops from the pressure tearing the surface wood fibers. Use the lowest amount of pressure needed to do the job; start off with a low pressure and adjust it upwards as needed.

Use a 1500 psi Power Washer or Less

Extremely high pressure is not necessary since you run the risk of tearing up the wood surface and leaving it with a "fuzzy" or "hairy" condition. This will not hurt the performance of the deck finish, but it can be objectionable in appearance, especially on decks.

Use a Low-Foaming Detergent

When power washing, use one of these three cleaning agents for optimal cleaning:

1. **Peroxide Bleach** like CPR.
2. **Bleach and Water** A mixture of 1 part household bleach and 5 parts water, plus 1 tablespoon TSP (trisodium phosphate) cleaner (optional). Chlorine bleach is NOT environmentally friendly and can be destructive to the wood if it remains on wood too long.
3. **Oxalic Acid** like X-180.

The detergent will assist the high pressure of the water in loosening and lifting all surface residues, including mill glaze. Use hot water for power washing and then rinse with cold water to flush all remaining detergent from the deck surface. A garden hose works really well for this. Regardless of which cleaning agent you use, make sure that it is thoroughly rinsed away.

When using products like CPR or X-180, be sure to follow the instructions as listed either on the can, or on the accompanying literature.

Use a Fan Spray Nozzle

Apply the water at an angle so it does not spray back into your face (be sure to wear safety goggles). Hold the nozzle at a distance, just far enough away from the surface to avoid "fuzzing" up the outer layer of wood. At this distance, the water and detergent will impact the wood with tremendous force and will remove virtually all residues, as well as creating considerable micro-roughening of the surface for enhanced stain penetration. If fuzzing occurs, the wood will need to be lightly sanded down with 3M pads or an Osborn buffing brush once the wood has thoroughly dried. Read more about power washing on pages 94–95.

New decks can be media blasted with cob, sand, glass, or soda, though media blasting is not typically recommended. Media blasting works well for decks where you want to remove a prior finish; for new decks, it is just an unnecessary expense.

For Previously Finished Decks and Railing

Finishes that are chipping and peeling will need to be removed. Depending on the condition of the finish, you may only need to power wash in order to remove the finish. If power washing fails to completely remove the finish, a paint stripper or media blasting is recommended.

Paint strippers are potentially the most caustic remedy for finish removal and are not recommended if your deck is situated near rivers, lakes, and streams. If you choose to strip the deck finish, be aware that there are environmentally friendly products on the market that will strip both oil- and water-based finishes. Once applied, the finish can be washed off with a garden hose. See more about chemical strippers on page 99.

Media blasting with cob, sand, or soda is a viable alternative to chemical stripping. If you decide to have your deck and rails blasted, be sure to have the work done by a seasoned professional who has had experience with decks and rails. An inexperienced novice can do severe, irreparable damage. Read more about media blasting on pages 96–98.

For deck finishes that are fading and wearing away without chipping or peeling, a simple washing with soap and water may be all that is needed before applying a recoat. If this fails to remove all of the dirt, grease, and finish residue, a light power washing with CPR, bleach and water and a little TSP, or X-180 should be used. X-180 is a great product for removing oil and grease stains around the barbecue area.

Once the decks and rails have been either stripped or cleaned, allow the wood to dry. If media blasting or power washing was done, you may need to do some additional sanding to smooth out any rough areas. Sanding debris can either be rinsed off with a garden hose or blown away with compressed air.

Make sure that the deck and rails are thoroughly dry before refinishing. Then apply a new coat of deck finish following the manufacturer's guidelines. Remember that finishes applied to wood that is too wet, hot, or cold will have adhesion problems and will fail much earlier. Once the deck has been recoated, allow the deck finish to fully cure before using it. Again, follow the guidelines as stated by the manufacturer.

Deck Finish Problem Solving

Fading Deck Finish

This deck had been coated with a penetrating oil-based deck finish high in paraffinic oils. This type of finish soaks deeply into the wood grain without building up a heavy coating on the surface of the wood. Exposure to the elements and general foot traffic will eventually wear the finish down. This is considered natural wear and is inevitable with this type of finish.

Photo 1 shows where exposure to direct sunlight for long periods of time has done the most damage to the deck finish. You can see in Photo 2 where the sheltered area of the deck has held up substantially better then the exposed areas in Photo 1.

In Photo 3 the areas left and right of the deck post show the difference in fading that can result from varying degrees of direct and indirect sun exposure.

Photo 4 shows damage to the finish on the steps, caused by typical, day-to-day foot traffic.

Treatment
Because there is not a heavy surface buildup of finish, the deck can be washed down with a mild detergent to remove any loose pigment or debris and, when dry, it can be recoated with deck finish.

Photo 1. Finish exposed to direct sunlight.

Photo 2. Finish under sheltered entryway.

Photo 3. Fading difference on both sides of post.

Photo 4. Finish wear due to normal foot traffic.

The deck is washed down and rinsed in sections. Warm water, a mild detergent, and a synthetic-bristled broom are all that is necessary. The deck should be thoroughly rinsed. Remove all debris from cracks.

Deck Finish Flaking Off

Deck finishes that build up a heavy surface coating will eventually break down and start to chip, peel, and flake off. This condition can be accelerated if the deck finish was originally applied when the deck was too damp or if the temperature was either too hot or too cold. Deck furniture that is dragged across the deck will tear at the finish coating and accelerate breakdown.

Treatment

Power wash the deck to remove the loose and flaking finish and dirt. See *Power Washing Logs* on pages 94–95. Once the deck is power washed, allow the deck to dry. Complete any additional sanding if necessary and then recoat with the manufacturer-recommended number of coats of finish.

If power washing proves ineffective, the deck will have to be either stripped or media blasted. Read more about other options on pages 96–99.

Once the deck is prepped for finishing, be sure to follow the manufacturer's guidelines for either recoating or applying a new finish.

Closeup of peeling and flaking deck finish.

Damage to Exposed Log Railing

The tops of railing that is exposed to the sun and physical contact will wear down and need to be recoated. Horizontal checks can open in the railing and allow rainwater into the wood, causing rot to set in if not repaired.

Prevention

Log railing should be treated with a borate wood preservative like PeneTreat prior to finishing. A clear finish should not be used on railing. A semi-transparent finish will provide longer lasting protection from seasonal wear. Make sure that checks are properly sealed with caulking. Periodic observation of the condition of railing will minimize the possibility of serious damage to the rails.

Treatment

Generally, you can just sand down the damaged areas and recoat with finish. If damage is extensive and rot has set in, the infected rail could be replaced with

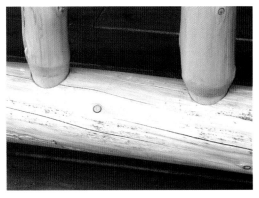

Fungus starting to grow on a lower railing due to backsplashing from the deck. Water will enter spindle holes. The holes should be sealed or another type of connection should be used. Joints should shed water and not hold water.

new railing. Another treatment would be to install impel rods (pages 138–139) along the underneath of the railing to treat against rot and the possibility of insect damage. WoodEpox and LiquidWood (pages 134–137) may be used as well to repair damage to the rail.

Log Rot on Exposed Deck Post

This post shows rot that has taken place in the heartwood. Rot will develop as rainwater enters the openings in the wood. The water-laden core of the post will swell and cause additional checking and damage. Flat tops are always more of a problem then crowned tops.

Treatment

The soft, rotted, heartwood area of the post should be dug out with an awl or flat-headed screwdriver to determine how much rot has taken place. If the rot goes down just a few inches, mix up some PeneTreat or other borate wood preservative and saturate the interior of the cavity.

Allow the wood to dry and then mix up enough WoodEpox to fill the cavity. LiquidWood can be added in small amounts to the WoodEpox to thin it down. This will help the WoodEpox to soak into the wood fiber and adhere to the wall of the cavity. Fill with epoxy up to ½ inch to ¾ inch from the top of the post and allow to dry. Pigment can be mixed with WoodEpox to give the top ½ inch to ¾ inch of the plug some pigmentation. Use the pigmented epoxy plug to complete the patch.

Once dry, the WoodEpox can be sanded down and coated with finish. Any checks larger than ¼ inch will need backer rod inserted into the check and sealed with caulking. Caulking is a better material than WoodEpox for sealing checks. The checks will expand and contract and caulking will flex with the changes, whereas WoodEpox cures very hard and can crack and fall out over time. If the damage is more severe, replace the post with a new one.

Water Damage to Log Post

The cedar posts for this deck stair platform were cut flat with no endcoating (Sealtite 60, Anchor Seal, or a similar product) protection or vapor barrier between the wood and cement. Two of them were placed on a poured cement slab that had been water sealed. The other two were erected on cement tiles without any water sealant. The posts and decking were tested for the amount of moisture content and then professionally coated with Sashco's Capture and Cascade. The deck was completed; it looked great.

After about a year, the water damage became visible. The two posts on the untreated cement tiles were affected first. Water migrated through the unsealed tiles and moved upwards, into the cedar posts, spreading discoloring tannins through the grain. The Capture/Cascade combination finish worked well as a moisture resistant coating; unfortunately, it was keeping

Closeup of damage with algae growing in water blisters.

water in and not out. Blisters formed on the surface as the water tried to escape. The blisters didn't burst; they swelled with water and turned green from algae, then proliferated along the surface. If the post is not treated, it will eventually look bleached out and

Untreated water damage a year later.

Example of finish applied over untreated water damage. The log post will continue to absorb ground moisture, which will eventually rot the post from the inside out.

cracked as shown above. If the post is untreated with the exception of being recoated with finish, it will appear blotchy and the fungus will continue to grow. In time, the post will lose its structural stability.

Treatment

The blisters will have to be cut to allow the moisture to drain. The finish will then have to be removed from discolored portions of the post. Chemical strippers or power washing will work. Using a product like X-180 or another oxidizer can lighten the dark discoloration of the wood caused by tannins, but it is unlikely that it will be completely removed. A new replacement post will have to be installed if you want to remove all signs of discoloration.

The post must be allowed to dry out and then an endcoating can be used if the endgrain of the post is accessible. A vapor barrier such as a piece of rubber roofing membrane can then be cut to fit under the post and cap the endgrain and endcoating. The edges of the membrane should be sealed with a one-part urethane caulking such as Manus-Bond, Sikaflex, or Lexel.

Impel rods placed approximately 4 inches from the ground will help protect the posts in the future from rot and decay. A 1-inch lift would also help to keep water away from the endgrain. Another helpful step towards preventative maintenance would be to use a water seal on the concrete tiles.

Log Post and Stonework

The log post shown above has been anchored into exterior stonework. Though it's a creative use of log and stonework, the log post will begin to rot in the same way as the log post on pages 131–132.

Blowing rainwater will drip down the length of the post and collect on the stonework shelf that surrounds the post. The masonry cement that has been used around the post will absorb water like a sponge. The log post will, in time, begin absorbing water from the cement and rot will begin.

As the log post naturally expands and contracts, the masonry around it will begin to crack and crumble, making it even easier for rainwater to enter down into the log end. The fact that the end of the log is concealed beneath the stonework makes it difficult to monitor the condition of the wood and the extent of decay that may already be taking place.

Treatment

The top layer of stones should be removed so that the condition of the log end can be determined. Use a moisture meter to test the moisture content of the wood. Cover the area with a tarp to keep additional rainwater from absorbing into the post or stonework. When the wood has dried out, use an endsealer if possible. Insert impel rods to protect the end of the post from future decay.

Replace the stonework leaving a ¼-inch gap around the post to be sealed with caulking. Treat the surrounding stonework and masonry cement with waterproof sealer. Monitor the condition of the caulking and masonry cement sealer on a yearly basis, maintaining both as needed.

Chapter 9: Log Restoration

You can see where these logs had putty applied. The grain is smoother and there are differences in coloration. You can see that the work had been done a number of years ago by the deterioration of the log finish. The homeowner can easily do this type of repair.

Patching Rotted Wood

Rotted areas of logs and timbers can easily be patched with the appropriate material. The powdered wood putty that mixes with water is not the ideal material for log structures. Though fine for its intended use, this type of wood putty lacks the structural stability and flexibility necessary for repairing logs and timbers.

WoodEpox is a brand name for a two-part epoxy wood replacement compound that, once dried, is stronger than wood and can be used for exterior and interior wood. WoodEpox is ideal for replacing rotted or missing sections of wood, and for filling cracks and voids. It can also be stained, painted, sanded, planed, nailed, and drilled. Dry pig-

ments can be kneaded into WoodEpox during the mixing process. It is recommended that pigmented WoodEpox be used for at least the outside ½-inch surface shell where there will be sanding and planing.

LiquidWood is an epoxy in liquid form that penetrates deteriorated wood and then hardens after penetration. LiquidWood adds permanent reinforcement to deteriorated wood as it restores structural strength and is ideal for exterior and interior use. Like WoodEpox, it can be sanded, drilled, painted, and planed. It is also an effective primer for WoodEpox.

Wood Reconstruction

To repair the damaged end of this timber, the wood should first be saturated with PeneTreat or other borate wood preservative to protect it from future fungal attack and insect damage. Once the PeneTreat and timber have dried, LiquidWood can be brushed onto the semi-rotted wood with a paintbrush to add strength and stability. A heat gun or electric hair dryer can be used to speed up the drying time.

Nails are then spaced about 2 inches apart from each other and about ½ inch away from the new end. The nails will give reinforcement between the wood and the WoodEpox (similar to adding metal rebar to concrete).

A wooden form is then nailed around the end to mold the new sides. A mixture of LiquidWood and WoodEpox can be applied to the rough surface cavity of the previously rotted wood. This half-and-half mixture will absorb and coat the cavity more thoroughly than an application of WoodEpox alone.

An endcap will also be nailed to the form before the WoodEpox is added. The wooden endcap will give a wood texture to the WoodEpox. The WoodEpox is then mixed up and filled in and around the nails while the half-and-half WoodEpox/LiquidWood is still tacky. Be sure to use rubber gloves when handling WoodEpox.

Remove the form when the WoodEpox has thoroughly dried. Sand down any rough edges left from the form with a file or grinder and then stain or finish with the desired color.

An example of using sawdust and wood glue as a wood putty. This combination works well; however, it leaves a distinctive gritty surface.

These same basic steps can be used when patching areas on a log. Try to dig out as much of the rotted wood as possible from the infected area of the log before starting the patchwork. Log scrapers are useful for doing this kind of work and come in a variety of shapes and sizes.

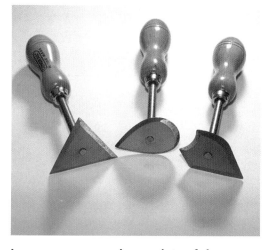

Log scrapers come in a variety of shapes and sizes, making it easy to dig out the rotted areas from logwork.

A Wooden Plug

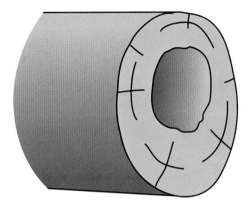

1. Use log scrapers to clean out all of the rotted wood from the log cavity.

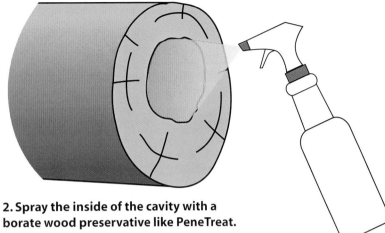

2. Spray the inside of the cavity with a borate wood preservative like PeneTreat.

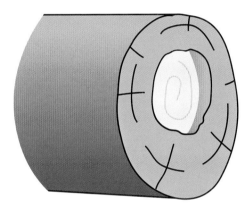

3. Once the preservative has dried, a mixture of WoodEpox and LiquidWood can be coated on the inside of the cavity. While the mixture is still tacky, WoodEpox can be added to the cavity.

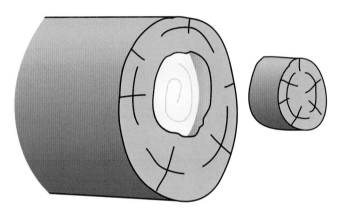

4. A dry, 2- to 3-inch wooden plug that has been treated with a borate wood preservative can now be inserted into the cavity.

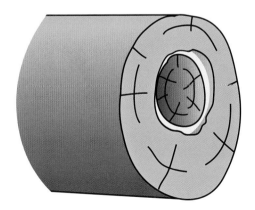

5. WoodEpox will be forced up and around the wooden plug as it is seated in place. Add or remove WoodEpox in order to allow a ½-inch space between the end of the plug and the end of the log.

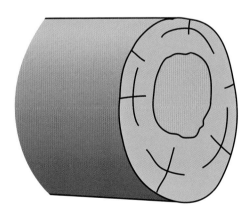

6. Mix powdered pigment with WoodEpox to cap the end and give a color similar to the log end. This will make the patch less noticeable when the log end is stained, once the patch has cured. Cut or sand the plug to match the appearance of the log end.

Borate Wood Preservatives

Borate wood preservatives like Boracol, Guardian, PeneTreat, Shell-Guard, or Timbor have proven to be an effective and environmentally safe method of controlling wood-destroying organisms, including wood boring insects like carpenter ants, beetles, and termites. Borates are also very toxic to brown rot and white rot fungi as well as over 45 other species of fungi.

Borate wood preservatives are non-toxic to humans and animals, odorless, and noncorrosive, and they do not change the color of wood. They are, however, toxic to plants and vegetation, so when applying them you should take care to cover or protect plants you don't want destroyed.

Borates are generally water-based and are available in powder form that you mix with water, or premixed in a liquid glycol solution. The preservative has to be applied to bare wood for it to properly penetrate the wood fibers so it is best applied to freshly peeled green logs. Due to its water-based nature, it can leach out of treated wood that is not protected from rain or rewetting with a water repellent finish or plastic tarp.

Borate preservatives are also very useful in log restoration work in the form of impel rods and as a preventative maintenance coating for many of the remedies discussed in the pages ahead.

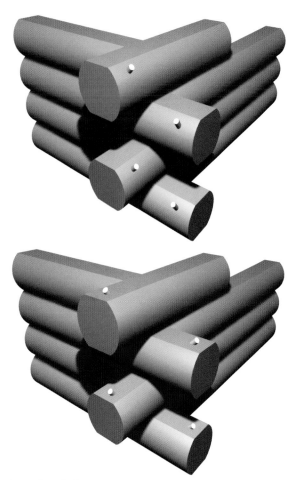

Impel rod placement shown on a butt and pass corner. Impel rods can be placed underneath the log ends to better conceal the rods.

Impel Rods

Log corners are highly susceptible to wood decay. Log homes that are less than six years old have been known to have serious premature decay affecting the corners and sill logs. The problems are generally caused by water backsplashing from improper house design. See *Design for Easy Maintenance* on pages 13–21 for additional information.

Impel rods are solid rods of concentrated boron that are inserted into holes drilled into log ends and along the length of the logs. The rods are activated when they come into contact with water. Boron and water make boric acid, which is an extremely safe inhibitor of wood-decaying fungi and acts as an insecticide. As water contacts the impel rods, the boric acid disperses to the wettest areas of the log end, providing protection to the most fungi-prone areas. The more moisture, the more the rod will diffuse into the wood.

Installation

Impel rods are available in various sizes to fit different applications. An 8-inch D-style log would take a 3 inch long by ¾ inch wide rod. Drill a 1³⁄₁₆-inch diameter hole 5 inches deep into the log end. The hole should be drilled so that the rod will be within 6 inches of the end of the log. The rods can be placed at various angles in the logs. See the placement diagram.

Once the rod is inserted, it should be covered with a ⅞ inch by 1½ inch wood plug, although caulking or wood putty can be substituted. In most cases, the rods can be inserted from underneath the log ends to hide the wooden plugs. It is important to note the need for the ½-inch space between the rod and the wood plug. The rods are highly

compressed and will swell when they come in contact with water.

An alternative to using impel rods is to make a paste out of water and the powdered borate preservative, and then apply this paste into holes bored into the logs. This method is helpful, though not nearly as effective as using impel rods due to the lack of concentration of boron in the applied paste.

Other Uses

Impel rods can also be used in sill logs (placed every 15 inches) and logs that abut window and door frames. They can be inserted into new log crowns to add future protection. They can be used on new construction as preventative maintenance. Why wait until the log ends have already rotted? Impel rods can be installed during construction and hidden from view in lateral joints as the house is being constructed.

Other areas where impel rods prove to be beneficial are in log posts, deck rails and spindles, and window and door jambs. Impel rods can also be installed in logs every 15 inches where backsplashing from decks occur. Anywhere that backsplashing affects logs, impel rods can be used.

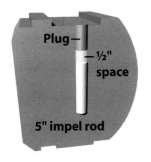

Position of Impel Rods

Diffusion of Impel Rods

Diffusion Complete

Rotted Log Ends with Gray Patina

and use WoodEpox to finish filling in around the plug and the cavity wall. You can also use LiquidWood and sawdust to create a paste to fill the cavity.

A charcoal-colored masonry pigment (available from masonry stores) can be used to color the WoodEpox. Add just enough of the pigment to color the WoodEpox gray like the rest of the building. Knead it in with the WoodEpox. Remember, you only have to color the last ½ inch of the end of the log. Once the plug has been inserted and the WoodEpox has cured, apply an end coating like Sealtite 60 to seal the ends of the wood.

To add strength and stability to the log ends without replacing them with new crowns: Drill 1 foot from the log end back horizontally into the more stable wood and use 1-foot lengths of fiberglass reinforcement rods to act as locking pins for internal strength. Use the LiquidWood as a glue around the rod. You should use at least three rods per log. To hide the ends of the rods, cut a wooden end-plug coated with a product called LifeTime. The LifeTime will turn the new wood gray to match the rest of the building.

For restoring log ends and maintaining the natural gray patina of logs, first, use a borate wood preservative like PeneTreat to saturate the logs and keep them from rotting any further. Next, use LiquidWood to seal cracks and create an undercoating for the WoodEpox to adhere to. Then, use new lumber or a piece of straight-grained salvaged or similar dry wood to cut a "plug" to fill the cavity.

Once the plug has been cut from the new stock, saturate the plug with PeneTreat to provide rot resistance. After the PeneTreat has dried, coat the plug with LiquidWood, insert the plug

Note: You can also spray the entire building with LifeTime finish to keep it gray. To add additional water resistance to the finish, you can use a product called DriSeal as a water protection coat for the building. Other products that would work well are Wood Guard and WR5 Clear.

Rotted Board and Batten Corner Panels

A practical device used over dovetail notches, especially the squared, non-self-draining style, were board and batten corner panels. The panels protected the exposed endgrain of the logs from the elements and added longevity to the corners. In time, when the panels had weathered and started to decay, they could easily be replaced with new ones before damage occurred to the house logs. Most often, the board and batten corners were pegged with wooden dowels to the sides of the structure.

Treatment 1

Remove the damaged corner boards and check the condition of the chinking around the notches. Repair chinking as needed. Replace boards with new ones.

Treatment 2

For those of you who would rather not cover the dovetail corners, an end coating such as Sealtite 60 can be applied to seal the endgrain of the exposed logs. This will help keep moisture out of the logs.

End coatings contain wax as part of the sealant so if you plan on finishing the logs, you should finish them first and then apply the end coating. Otherwise the end coating could cause adhesion problems with the finish, especially water-based finishes.

Apply chinking around the corner notches, using backer rod if necessary to complete the sealing process. For more information see *Backer Rod and Chinking Step-by-Step* on pages 50–61.

Chinked corner notches.

Log Crowns

Log ends can be successfully replaced when they have suffered serious rot and decay with a replacement end called a log crown. The damaged portion of the end is cut out and removed. A bevel is cut to increase surface area for the log crown as shown above. You can see the holes in the logs that were caused by rot, common in White Cedar; they can easily be plugged. It was determined that the rot had taken place while the tree was alive and that there is no ongoing rot taking place in this area of the log. Fortunately, the wood is structurally sound and void of moisture damage.

A new crown is shown being test fitted. Each crown is custom cut and scribed to fit. Crowns are often made from cedar for increased rot resistance.

Marking and Cutting the Bevel

If you are going to be replicating a log crown like that shown on the previous page to be attached to a beveled cut face, a few extra steps are necessary.

First, mark off the area to be removed from the rotted log crown. In the example shown, 6 inches will be left. Cut the log crown at the marked area leaving 6 inches of the existing log.

Using a ruler, find and mark the center of the cut end of the crown. From the center mark, use a straightedge to mark the log for the two bevel cuts. Use a chainsaw to cut the bevels.

Now that the existing log has been prepped for the new crown, turn your attention to the new crown log. Basically, you will be following the same steps to make the bevel cuts except that you will be working in the opposite direction.

Find and mark the center of the new crown. Measure the 6-inch distance and from that point, mark the bevels. The key to a tight fit is to use a crown log that is as close as possible to the circumference of the existing log.

Cut the reverse bevel from the log crown. If all of the cuts have been carefully measured and cut, the new crown should fit snugly onto the existing house log.

Bird's eye view illustrations of the bevel marking and cutting process.

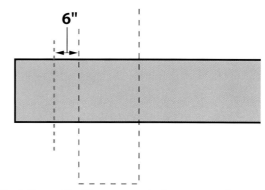

1. Mark the rotted log crown to be removed leaving 6 inches of solid wood.

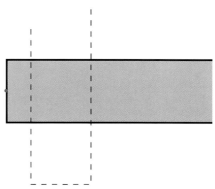

2. Use a ruler to find and mark the center of the log's circumference. Mark shown in red.

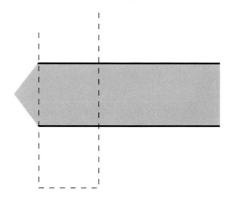

3. Mark and cut the bevels back from the centerline, removing the excess wood.

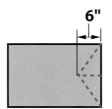

4. Using a ruler, mark the centerline of the circumference of the new crown. Measure out 6 inches from the centerline and mark the corresponding diagonal lines for cutting the reverse bevel from the new crown.

How to Scribe-Fit a New Crown

Scribing is the process of using a scriber to transfer the contoured edge of one surface onto another unconnected surface. The metal stylus is used to follow the contour that is to be transferred while the pencil marks the new surface. The easiest way to scribe is to do so in a two-step process. For scribing crowns, be sure that you use a scriber with levels that can be rotated so that the arms can be leveled horizontally as well as vertically.

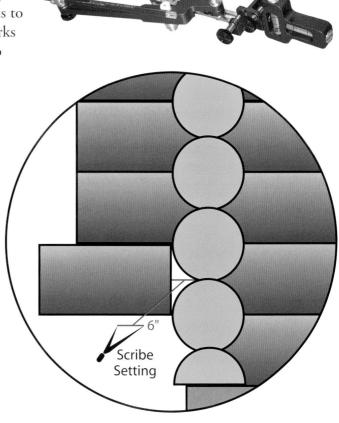

Step 1. The Rough Scribe

Rough scribing is necessary to mark and cut the ends of the crown so that it may be fitted within 2 inches of its final placement. To get started, make sure that the log that you have chosen is approximately the same diameter as the original log end and 8 inches to 10 inches longer. This extra length allows space on the crown in case you make a mistake and need to rescribe and recut numerous times. Also, the crown log should be thoroughly dry (19 percent moisture content or less) and free of rot and decay.

If the new crown is going in between other log crowns both above and below, wedges can be used to hold it in position while you scribe. If the new crown is to be placed as shown in the illustrations to the right, a sawhorse or other stationary structure will need to be in place to hold the new crown for proper scribing.

Place the new crown as close to the log notches as possible, Make sure that you keep it in line with the log that it is connecting to. Use the scriber to measure the space between the end of the crown and the deepest part of the notch. In the illustration, the distance happens to be 6 inches. We want to be within 2 inches of the final scribe, so deduct 2 inches from the 6-inch distance. Set the scriber arms to 4 inches (6 inches – 2 inches = 4 inches).

Next, make sure that the scriber level is properly set by placing both the pencil end and the stylus end on the edge of a

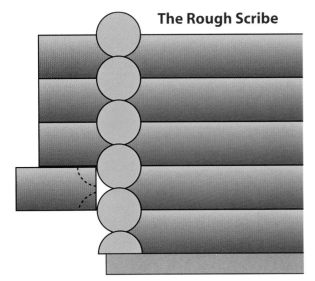

The Rough Scribe

horizontal level (make any adjustments if necessary). Once the scriber settings are finalized, make the rough scribe. Be sure that as you scribe, the scriber is held with the level marks always at level. The more level the scriber is held throughout the scribing process, the more accurate the scribe marks will be.

When you have finished scribing the new crown, remove the crown from its position and cut out the area of the crown that was scribed with a chainsaw. Be careful to saw as close as possible to the scribe lines.

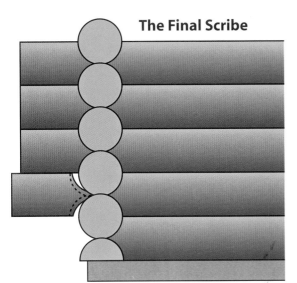

The Final Scribe

Step 2. The Final Scribe

Return the crown to the scribing position, placing it as close as possible to the log joinery. Set the scriber arms to the **farthest** distance between the log joinery and the newly notched log crown. This setting should be approximately 2 inches.

Recheck the scriber arms against the horizontal level to be sure that the scriber settings are still correct.

Now, make the final scribe on both sides of the log crown. Remember to keep both bubbles perfectly level as you scribe the log crown.

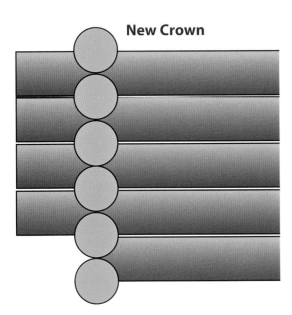

New Crown

Remove the crown from its position and carefully remove the excess wood from the final scribe-marked area with a chainsaw.

Reset the crown into position and check the fit. The crown should fit snugly into place. Any small gaps that exist between the crown and the logs can be filled with spray foam or backer rod and then caulked over.

Wedges are handy tools to help level and hold the new crown in place for marking, measuring, and fitting.

Scaffolding is necessary to provide safety and stability. It also makes it easy for two people to work, replacing crowns on both sides of a log wall.

Below, select cedar logs are chosen and expertly drawknifed and sawn to make the new log crowns. These logs must be free of rot and insect damage.

Once the crown is cut and fitted properly, it is set into place and then anchored in place with long lag screws.

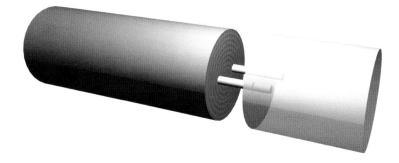

In areas that lack support, two fiberglass reinforcement rods can be used to align the crown and give strength and stability.

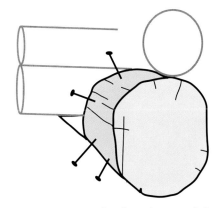

Lag screws are evenly placed around the new crown as shown above. The small screw heads are embedded just below the surface of the crown; caulking or WoodEpox is then used to seal over the screw heads.

The new log crown shown anchored in place. Care must be taken so that the circumference of the new crown matches the existing house log that it will be attached to. Slight variances in size can be adjusted by lightly grinding the oversized area with a hand-held grinder.

The next replacement crown is shown being marked and scribed for cutting and fitting.

Once all of the new crowns have been installed, they are caulked to prevent water from entering in cracks between the new crowns and the house logs.

Spray foam can also be used to fill in around irregularly spaced cracks and gaps. Once the spray foam has cured, excess foam is removed to provide a smooth appearance. Caulking is applied over the foam to completely seal the area from water infiltration.

Backer rod may be used instead of spray foam to fill gaps larger than ¼ inch deep. The backer rod, like the spray foam, should be caulked or chinked over to provide water resistance.

Half-Log Replacement

Half-log replacement is a cost-effective alternative to full log replacement, provided that only surface rot is present and the vast majority of the log is structurally sound and free of decay.

A reciprocating saw is used to cut out the half-log area to be removed. Slicks and electric planers can be used to flatten out the surface and do any necessary cleanup.

Often, the exposed wood and new half-log are coated with a borate preservative such as PeneTreat to help protect the wood from insects and future rot.

A half-log replacement is custom cut to match the area that was removed and is then anchored in place with log screws like OlyLog or BlueOx.

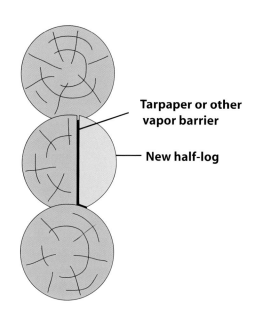

Tarpaper or other vapor barrier

New half-log

An option when installing half-logs is to place tarpaper or other vapor barrier material between the house log and new half-log. The barrier will prevent water from penetrating into the house log, adding extra protection from future rot damage.

The new half-log is test fitted to ensure a proper fit. Notice how the right end of the half-log has been notched to fit behind the window frame.

A new half sill log has been installed and the edges sealed with spray foam. Once the foam has cured, the excess foam will be trimmed off and then sealed with caulking.

Full-Log Replacement

When rot and/or insect damage is so severe that more than fifty percent of the log is structurally unsound, the entire log will need to be replaced. The log walls will need to be jacked up for removal and replacement. Usually it is the sill logs and one or two logs above that need replacing. However, depending on the circumstances, any number of logs, regardless of their position in the stacking order, may need replacement.

Jacking up log walls can be a dangerous process because logs can tilt and roll out from their notched positions causing a serious safety hazard, as well as damaging the notches and requiring additional repair. If the jacks are not placed properly to distribute the load of the house, the notches can also be seriously damaged from overloading them. The logs can also become damaged from denting and scarring if the work is not done carefully.

Log buildings that are constructed with spikes or lag screws add another level of complexity to the log replacement process. The lags or spikes will have to be severed before the log can be fully removed and this will hamper the jacking process. The same is true of thru-bolts that run where the log in question must be removed. In most log replacement cases, a qualified restoration contractor should be called in.

For those of you who are interested in tackling such a project, be sure that you have all of the necessary tools listed before starting the project, and then proceed carefully.

Jacks The size of the house is of course a factor when determining the number and size of jacks needed. For a typical log building, three or four jacks in the 5- to 10-ton range are probably all that are necessary. A jack that fails during a crucial time can be disastrous, if not deadly, so it is always better to have a jack that is too big for the job rather than one that is too small.

Plank Carriage This is basically a bolt plate made from ¾-inch threaded rods, nuts, and four 2-by-12s or other large timbers (two for each side of the log wall per jack). The threaded rods act as lifting pins to spread and carry the weight of the log wall as it is being jacked. It also aids in keeping the wall logs from tipping and rolling out from their notches. The plank carriage is very useful when lifting wall logs while keeping the floor of the building intact. Otherwise, a portion of the flooring would have to be removed.

The plank carriage idea can also be used to lift log walls by spiking the 2-by-12s flush with door jamb (after removing the door). In most cases, the jacking of the logs is to take the pressure off the surrounding logs so that the rotted log can be removed, and it may only take ¼ inch of lift to allow the log to be loosened and/or cut out from its position.

Blocking and Wedges A supply of different sizes of blocks and wedges should be available to assist while the log wall is being jacked. Wedges are useful for distributing the weight of the wall while the blocks are used to

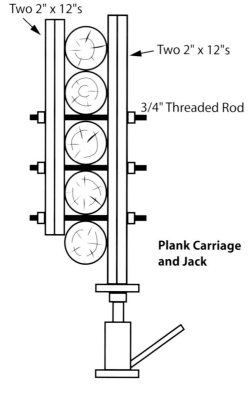

Two 2" x 12"s

Two 2" x 12"s

3/4" Threaded Rod

Plank Carriage and Jack

elevate jacks, stabilizing them from sinking into soft ground, and holding up portions of logs for stability.

Pry Bars 5-foot to 6-foot steel pry bars are useful in some situations to separate logs so that wedges can be tapped into place in order to spread the load of the house or to fit the threaded rods of the plank carriage into position. This step will not be necessary if the log building is a chink style house; once the chinking is removed there is adequate space between the logs for the threaded rod.

Come-Along This is a useful tool in some instances where multiple logs need to be replaced from the sill log up and there are windows on that side of the building. The come-along can be blocked to hold replacement logs in position below the older logs above, while the next log is being fitted.

Chainsaw An absolute necessity for cutting out portions of decayed logs and preparing replacement logs.

When cutting out logs that are spiked or lagged, use two chains—an older, dull one and a sharp one. Use the dull chain first to cut through and find the spikes or lags. Once the metal fasteners have been located and removed with a reciprocating saw, the sharp chain can be used to quickly finish cutting out the old log.

Other tools that will be needed include scriber, pencils, level, and tape measure. A reciprocating saw may be necessary to cut through spikes, lag screws, and thru-bolts. Safety equipment such as hard hats, eye protection, and work gloves is recommended.

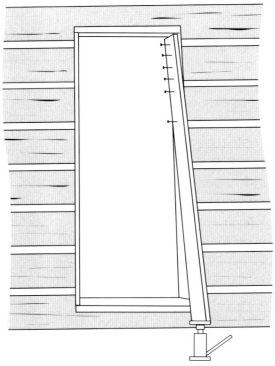

2-by-12 plank spiked to door jamb that can be jacked up to help relieve pressure from the logs.

Before you begin, take a careful assessment of the condition of the logs and overall layout of the building. Note how the floor joists are connected to the sill logs and how they may affect log replacement. Consider what electrical wiring and plumbing may need to be disconnected or removed so as not to interfere or cause harm when the log replacement work begins.

Log buildings carry the load of their weight primarily at the corners and down along the door and window jambs. Keep this in mind when you set the placement of the jacks.

The basics of jacking up a log building and replacing a log are simple: place jacks above the log to be removed, jack up building just enough to slide or cut out old log, insert new scribed log, lower the logs back down on top of new log and remove jacks. It is applying these basics to the real world circumstances of your particular situation that can become problematic.

Knowing where to place jacks is dependent on which log is to be removed. Usually, the jacks and plank carriages are placed within 2 feet to 3 feet of corner notches. Wedges are used to spread the weight of the building out to the wall logs and relieve pressure from the corner notches. Jacking and insertion of wedges should be done slowly and simultaneously so that the weight transfer from the notches is distributed gradually.

One of the easiest types of log buildings to jack up is the dovetail style. The large chink gaps between logs makes it easy to remove the chinking and insert the threaded rods of a plank carriage.

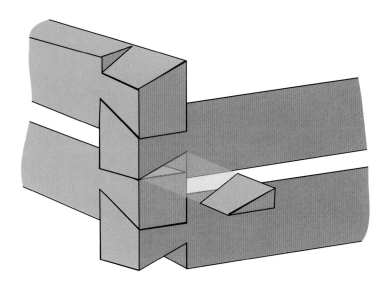

Cutting out the dovetail "key" to simplify log removal. The replacement log can be installed the same way by cutting off the key, sliding the log into place and then setting the key back into place and adhering it with WoodEpox.

By cutting out the key locking portion of the dovetail with a reciprocating saw, the entire log can easily be slid out.

To replace a new dovetail log, the old log can be used to pattern the notches for the new log. Once the new replacement log is ready to be put into place, the building needs only to be jacked up enough for the dovetail notches to fit into place. An alternative would be to insert the new log in the same manner that the old one was removed. First, cut off the key portion of the notch and slide it into place. Then, glue and reinsert the key back into the notch with WoodEpox.

Log replacement on premilled, kit homes can be done a little differently. Premilled logs are of varying lengths and stacked brick-like throughout the wall so that butted logs are overlapped with solid lengths of other logs. This makes it easy to replace logs by tapping in metal shims to allow enough room for a reciprocating saw to cut out a section of the log. A hydraulic or scissors jack can then be fitted into the space to lift up the wall enough to cut spikes or lag screws with a reciprocating saw and free the damaged log. Wood blocking can be inserted to help stabilize the area while a replacement log of the same size and profile can be set into place. The new log can be toenailed into position with spikes, but log screws like those made by Olympic are much faster and easier to install.

If the log section to be replaced is in conjunction with a thru-bolt, the new log can be channel notched to conceal the thru-bolt. Ideally, the splice would be at the location of a thru-bolt. If this is not possible, the thru-bolt could be severed and capped off. If you live in an area where your local building codes require thru-bolting for log homes, a channel notch will be required.

Replacing a damaged log on a premilled log home by inserting sections of logs.

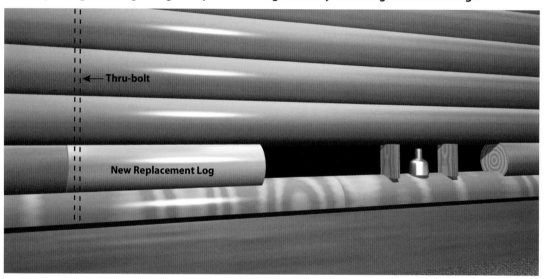

The final log section can be slid into place with the aid of metal shims hammered into postion to allow enough clearance for the last log to be set into place.

Plank carriages are used on this small cabin to allow rotted logs to be removed and replaced.

Progress is made with a combination of half-log and full-log replacements.

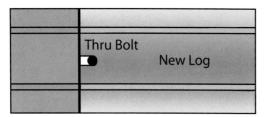

Bird's eye view of new milled log, channel notched to conceal a thru-bolt.

Log replacement of hand scribed log homes requires knowledge of scribing and notch cutting techniques. The same basic two-step scribing principles for log crowns apply to full-log replacement. See *How to Scribe Fit A New Crown* starting on page 144.

Because of the handcrafted nature of scribed log homes, be sure to take your time with the scribing and notching so that the replacement logs will not look like replacement logs.

To learn more about log construction techniques and principles, check out these books:

Log Construction Manual by Robert Chambers (Deep Stream Press).

Handbook of Canadian Log Building by F. Dan Milne (Muir Publishing Company Limited).

Notches of All Kinds by B. Allan Mackie (Firefly Books, Inc.).

See *Recommended Reading* on page 171 for more.

The corner notches are braced into position so that work can be done replacing the sill logs. Notice where the rotted log ends have been removed for new crown replacement.

The Problem with Painted Logs

Rainwater backsplashing from the entryway and railing has accelerated the painted logs' rot. In this situation, the overhead raingutter offered little protection. A sheltered entryway would have been beneficial.

This house was originally coated with house paint instead of a log home finish. You can see where the logs have cracked or "checked," leaving open cracks in the paint for rainwater to penetrate into the wood, causing rot. The density of the paint coating acts like a plastic sheeting that traps in moisture, causing water blisters and flaking paint.

In the wintertime when the logs freeze, the trapped moisture expands by becoming ice particles. This causes more subsurface damage, making tiny cracks larger and allowing more space for water to penetrate farther into the log, causing still more damage.

In a situation like this all of the paint needs to be removed with either a chemical stripper or sand- or cob blasting. The next step is to cut out the rotted areas of wood and use PeneTreat to saturate the logs and keep them from rotting any further. If the rotted areas are relatively shallow, LiquidWood can be used to seal cracks and create an undercoating for the WoodEpox to adhere to. Next, apply the WoodEpox and form it so that it conforms to the rest of the log. Then apply a new finish.

If large portions of the logs are rotted away, you will either have to replace portions of the log with half-log inserts or replace the entire log. You may need the services of a professional log restoration contractor.

Another painted log house with severe damage to the lower logs. Backsplashing from shrubbery too close to the house was the cause of much of the problem. The logs were restored by a combination of full-log, half-log, and log crown replacement.

Half-log siding is used to re-side the log cabin once the rotted areas have been cut out and treated with a preservative.

Though this is not a typical solution, the owner of the log cabin decided to side over the damage with half-log siding. The rotted areas of wood should first be cut out and any exposed wood treated with a borate preservative like PeneTreat. Any insect infestation must be addressed before new siding can be installed.

Windows will need to have jamb extensions added for the additional thickness of the new paneling, as will any outlets or vents. Furring strips will also need to be installed to provide a flat nailing area for the paneling.

The log ends could be cut back, treated with a borate wood preservative and then capped with board and batten corners to protect the notches from the elements.

To maintain the log cabin appearance, the new half-log siding could be scribe-fit to the log ends. To do this, scribe fit the two sides next to the log ends first, and then cut and fit the middle section of the paneling.

3. Make sure that the roof has proper ventilation. Check the condition of roof vents, ridge vents, soffits, and louvered areas to ensure that they are not blocked. With the vents free of obstructions, the roof will be able to stay free of heat and moisture buildup in the attic area and ice dams in the winter months will be minimized.

4. Apply a wood preservative finish to help protect the shakes or shingles. There are a number of finishes on the market designed for cedar roofs. Products like X-100 and WR-5 are for homeowners who wish to keep the shakes or shingles from graying or discoloring. How often you need to reapply a wood preservative treatment will be dependent on factors including your geographic location, condition of the cedar, type of preservative used, and the amount of shade and direct sunlight the roof receives. A good rule of thumb is to reapply every five years.

Before cleaning or treating the roof, check the overall condition of the shakes or shingles. If the roof has discolored and turned gray or darkened, it can easily be cleaned up to renew the golden cedar appearance. Signs of cupping, checking, and splitting are signals that the roof is deteriorating and needs to be either repaired or replaced.

When to Repair

This is a rather subjective situation, but the rule of thumb is to not repair shingle roofs that are older than 20 years and shake roofs that are older than 25 years. In coastal states that receive heavy rainfall like Washington and Oregon, repairing shingle roofs over 10 years and shake roofs older than 15 years is not recommended.

Another rule of thumb for when to replace a cedar shake or shingle roof: replace if more than 30 shakes or shingles need repairing per 100 square feet of roofing.

To Remove a Damaged Shake or Shingle

Use a short prybar to pry up the damaged shake and the shakes directly above the damaged one just enough to access the nails with a hacksaw or wirecutters. Using a hacksaw blade or wire cutters, cut the exposed nails from the damaged shake. Remove the damaged shake and retrieve the nails using pliers or a pair of vise-grips.

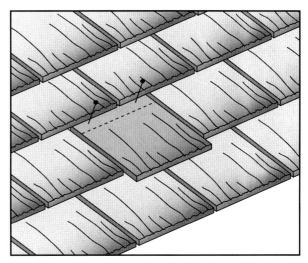

A new shake is slid into place ½ inch lower than the shakes next to it. Nails are driven into the shake at a 45-degree angle.

To Replace a Damaged Shake or Shingle

After the shake has been removed or if one is already missing, slide a new shake of proper size into the empty space. Allow the new shake to protrude ½ inch beyond the other shakes and nail in two nails at a 45-degree angle. Set the nails with a punch. With the nails hammered in flush to the new shake, use a hammer and a wooden block to tap the shake ½ inch back to its final resting place in line with the other shakes.

To Repair a Damaged Shake or Shingle

An alternative to removing and replacing damaged shakes is to insert a corrosion resistant metal shim underneath the damaged shake. The shim should be 2½ inches wide and about ½ inch longer than the shake or shingle that it is repairing. The end corners need to be bent downwards at a 45-degree angle to help hold it in place. Insert the shim all the way beneath the damaged shake so that the shim is hidden out of view. Shims can last as long as the roofs themselves.

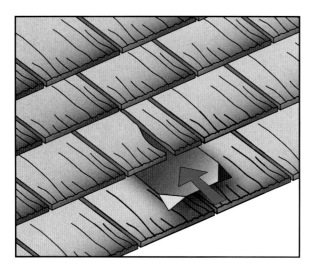

Clean with Bleach and Water

If the shakes are discolored from photodegradation due to UV damage from the sun, algae, and surface mildews, use a bleach and water solution for cleaning.

When cleaning with bleach, protect plants and shrubbery from the bleach solution and overspray. Plastic tarps are effective for covering and protecting vegetation; however, rinsing the vegetation before, during, and after bleaching

will minimize the need to cover plants and shrubbery.

Be mindful of where the rinse water is going to run off to. If you are near open bodies of water, you may want to power wash the roof without using a bleach solution, or substitute the bleach with a more environmentally friendly product.

A mixture of 1 part household bleach and 1 part water is recommended. A stronger solution can be made by using granular bleach like the kind available from swimming supply stores. Use 2 to 4 ounces of granular bleach for each gallon of water. Use warm water to dissolve the granular bleach.

Apply the bleach and water solution with a garden pump-sprayer at a rate of 1 to 1½ gallons per hundred square feet of roof area. Allow the solution to sit for 15 to 30 minutes before thoroughly rinsing with a garden hose or power washer. Rinsing with a power washer will not only remove the bleach and water solution but also leaves, dirt, debris, and rust stains.

Clean by Power Washing

Some forms of algae, lichen, and moss are impervious to bleach and must be removed physically with the aid of a power washer. To power wash, use 1,000 to 1,500 psi and a fan spray tip. This is a good pressure range to use, though experienced professionals use much higher pressures.

High pressure washing can be highly destructive to wood surfaces so it is always a good rule of thumb for the novice to use the lowest pressure necessary to get the job done.

Start at the ridgeline of the roof and work downwards using cold water. Hot water is considered unnecessary as are cleaning agents, however, cleaning products like X-180 can speed up the cleaning process. Hold the spray wand about a foot away from the shakes and keep the spray wand moving back and forth as you wash the shakes. This will minimize uneven wear marks on the shakes caused by excessive pressure.

Work Safety

Walking around on a wet cedar roof or stepping on a loose shake or shingle can be hazardous. Footwear should have non-slip soles; rubber logger boots with metal studs called "corkers" are recommended. When walking on shakes or shingles, walk across the roof instead of up and down.

OSHA-approved fall protection equipment including a safety harness, lanyards, and roofing brackets is also recommended. When using harsh chemicals like bleach, wear proper eye and hand protection. Rubber gloves and safety goggles are recommended. Avoid breathing in bleach vapors. If necessary, wear a safety respirator to protect your lungs.

A good quality ladder that extends about 3 feet beyond the roof eaves is also a good idea. The extra length of ladder makes accessing the roof easier and provides more stability. Don't try to carry your tools with you on the ladder. Use a 5-gallon bucket on a rope to safely lift tools up once you are on the roof.

If you feel concerned or uneasy about doing the work yourself, hire a professional to do the work for you.

Choosing a Professional

When choosing a professional to provide roof cleaning, application of wood treatments, or roof replacement, ask a few questions. Ask for references (including the Better Business Bureau, the Chamber of Commerce, and local consumers), and a workmanship guarantee. Also inquire about the type and brand of wood treatment that they apply. Products containing unfortified linseed oil, diesel fuel, crankcase oil, or those that make claims of fire retardancy should be avoided.

Ask the contractors if you can view other local roofs that they have washed and treated, or replaced—both recently and a few years earlier. This simple request will help you to avoid fly-by-night operators who travel around the country either gouging consumers with overinflated charges or underbidding local competitors and providing substandard work.

Ask to see their workers' compensation certificate. The homeowner may be liable for a workman who is injured at your home if the contractor has not paid his/her workers' compensation account.

For additional help in locating a qualified wooden roof installer or maintenance contractor, contact the Cedar Shake and Shingle Bureau (see *Resources* on page 170).

Resources

American Building Restoration, Inc.
9720 S. 60th St.
Franklin, WI 53132
800-346-7532 or 414-421-4125
Fax: 414-421-8696
Website: www.abrp.com

Cedar Shake and Shingle Bureau
P.O. Box 1178
Sumas, WA 98295-1178
604-820-7700
Fax: 604-820-0266
Website: www.cedarbureau.com

Continental Products
1150 E. 222nd St.
Euclid, OH 44117
800-305-5869 or 216-531-0710
Fax: 216-289-1745
Website: www.continentalprod.com

ISK Biocides, Inc.
416 E. Brooks Rd.
Memphis, TN 38109
Phone: 800-238-2523 or 901-344-5350
Fax: 901-344-5387
Website: www.woodguard.com

International Logbuilders' Association
P.O. Box 775
Lumby, British Columbia V0E 2G0 Canada
800-532-2900 or 250-547-8776
Website: www.logassociation.org

Menco Corporation
3600 E. Bacon Rd.
Hillside, MI 49242-0188
800-972-7693
Website: www.menco.com

Nixalite of America Inc.
1025 16th Ave.
East Moline, IL 61244
888-624-1189
Fax: 888-624-1196
Website: www.nixalite.com

Perma-Chink Systems, Inc.
1605 Prosser Rd.
Knoxville, TN 37914
800-524-3040
Website: www.permachink.com

Olympic Manufacturing Group
153 Bowles Rd. / P.O. Box 508
Agawam, MA 01001
800-633-3800
Fax: 413-789-1069
Website: www.olyfast.com

Sansin Corporation
3377 Egremont Dr.
R.R.#5 (Hwy. 22)
Strathroy, Ontario N7G 3H6 Canada
519-245-2001
Fax: 519-245-4759
Website: www.sansin.com

Sashco
10300 E. 107th Pl.
Brighton, CO 80601
800-767-5656
Fax: 303-286-0400
Website: www.sashco.com

Saver Systems
1751 Sheridan St.
Richmond, IN 47374
800-860-6327 or 765-966-5084
Fax: 317-935-4999
Website: www.saversystems.com

Schroeder Log Home Supply
Distribution Warehouses in IN, MN, SD, TN
1107 SE 7th Ave. / P.O. Box 864
Grand Rapids, MN 55744-0864
800-359-6614 or 218-326-4434
Fax: 800-755-3249
Website: www.loghelp.com

Sun Country Log Home Store
P.O. Box 1525
McMinnville, OR 97128
800-827-1688 or 503-324-0922
Fax: 503-324-3712
Website: www.loghomestore.com

Weatherall Company
106 Industrial Way
Charlestown, IN 47111
800-367-7068
Fax: 812-256-2344
Website: www.weatherall.com

Woodcare Systems
751 Kirkland Ave.
Kirkland, WA 98033
800-827-3480 or 425-827-6000
Fax: 425-822-5800
Website: www.woodcaresystems.com

Wood-Mizer Products, Inc.
8180 W. 10th St.
Indianapolis, IN 46214
800-553-0182 or 317-271-1542
Website: www.woodmizer.com

Recommended Reading

Log Construction

Building a Log Home from Scratch or Kit
Dan Ramsey (TAB Books). Learn how to prepare your own logs or buy your home in kit form, how to design, build and maintain, how to estimate construction costs, select materials, prepare the building site, erect walls, roof, and finish.

Building with Logs
B. Allan Mackie (Firefly Books Inc.). Well-written and -illustrated textbook. A standard text for log builders for over 30 years.

The Craft of Log Building
Hermann Phleps (Lee Valley Tools Ltd.). Translated from German, this outstanding book is one of the most important volumes on log building available in the northern hemisphere. A classic in Germany, this is the master work of Hermann Phleps, an architect and teacher of the art of timberwork for nearly 60 years.

Handbook of Canadian Log Building
F. Dan Milne. Packed with over 120 full color photos and 68 precise, black and white illustrations, this book takes the reader through log home construction step by step, with chapters on roof systems, electrical work, plumbing, installation of doors and windows, and more.

Log Construction Manual
Robert W. Chambers. Written by the co-author of "Log Building Standards," the building code for handcrafted log homes included in the back of this book. This is the information you need to help you build your own log home: detailed, helpful tricks of the trade by an experienced log builder and teacher.

The Log Home Guide Book: "Your Dreams Are Safe in Our Hands"
Gary Schroeder. An invaluable resource tool for the log home buyer or builder. Among its features, this volume offers special articles that explore what's happening in the log home industry today. This publication maintains its stellar reputation by combining consumer advocacy with straight talk and helpful facts.

Log Span Tables
Mackie, Read, and Hahney (International Log Builders Association). Newly updated and expanded data for calculation of correct sizes of logs for log construction, plus log building standards.

Notches of All Kinds
B. Allan Mackie (Firefly Books Inc.). Photos and drawings showing all kinds of timber joinery. Great reference book.

Maintenance & Restoration

Building and Restoring the Hewn Log House
Charles McRaven (Betterway Books). Valuable instruction on foundations, framing the house, hewing the logs, replacing rotted wood, notching the corners, and various other information needed to build or restore the hewn log house.

Common-Sense Pest Control
William and Helga Olkowski, Sheila Daar (The Taunton Press). Proven and practical solutions to a variety of household and garden pests.

The Log Home Owner's Manual
Jim Renfroe (Advantage Entertainment). A guide to protecting and restoring exterior wood. A good reference guide for log home owners, covering insects, wood rot, preservatives, pressure washing, sapstain, application of wood finishes, decks, cedar shakes, and much more.

Log Structures Preservation and Problem-Solving
Harrison Goodall and Renee Friedman (American Association for State and Local History). With an emphasis on historic preservation, the information applies to any type of log construction or renovation.

Renovating Barns, Sheds, and Outbuildings
Nick Engler (Storey Books). From the foundation up, this book shows how to save money, history, and architecture when you renovate or restore, rather than replace.

Renovating Old Houses
George Nash (The Taunton Press). A book about fixing up those fixer uppers, written for homeowners who want professional results and for professionals who are serious about renovation. All areas of the house are covered from foundations to roofs.

Restoring Wooden Houses
Nigel Hutchins (Firefly Books Inc.). Packed with practical information. The author offers advice on everything from the proper approach to restoration, historical research, and ways of contracting the job, to care and protection of wood, paint stripping, and much more.

Reviving Your House
Alan Dan Orme (Storey Books). Five hundred inexpensive and simple solutions to basic home maintenance issues. A great manual for the homeowner.

Squirrel Proofing Your Home and Garden
Rhonda Massingham Hart (Storey Books). Learn how to understand and control squirrels, chipmunks, groundhogs, and other squirrel relatives.

Index

water protection coatings, 140
water-based, 85
for wooden roofs, 167
fire damage restoration, 98, *98*
flashing
on chimneys, *21*
of decking, *20, 26*
on dormers, 19
on gables, 67
leakage at, 29
materials for, 21
flat-headed wood borers, 30, 36–37, *36*
flies, 31, 40–41
floodlights, 46
fly swatters, 36, 41
Foam Weld (adhesive), 51
follow plate, 55, 57
footwear, 169
foundations
drainage from, 13
inspections for, 23
inspections of, 26
vegetation adjacent, 15, *161*
fruiting bodies (fungus), 26
full-log replacement, *157, 161*
jack placement and use, 155
jacking door jambs, *154*
jacking log building, 155
jacking up log walls, 153
tools for, 153–154
fungicides, 10, 33
fungus. *See also* sapstain fungus
from backsplashing on railing, *129*
from cob blasting, 97
damage by, 85
fruiting bodies, 26
in posts, with untreated ends, 132
furniture beetles, 37

glass blasting, 96
gray colorant, 140
green logs, 10, 70
grinder, hand-held, 148
Grip Strip (backer rod), 50–51, *50, 52, 52*
ground contact/moisture
log posts and, 14
sill logs and, 13, 25, *25*, 116
termites, 40
wood to soil clearances, 40, 116
Guardian (borate preservative), 138
gutters

backsplash problems, 113, 114
maintenance of, 29, 114, 166
need for, 19, 115

half-log replacement, *157, 161*
installation of, *151*
log restoration, 150, *150*
spray foam, *151*
half-log siding, 162, *162*
Handbook of Canadian Log Building
(Milne), 158
health hazards. *See* safety
heartwood, 9
horizontal log joints, 65
horntails (insects), 31, 41
house fires, 44

Impel Rods
backsplash problems, 19, 115
for ground contact sill logs, 116
installation and use, 138–139
in log posts, 132, 133
in log railings, 129
for old unfinished logs, 100
placement of, *138, 139*
in vertical log joints, 66
incompatibility (finishes), 85, 92, 104, *104*
inner bark, 12, 103, *103*
insecticides, 35, 36, 84. *See also*
borate preservatives; CPF-2D
insects, 68
chinking damage, *68*
control of, 34, 115
general treatment of, 32
inspections for, 22, 23
shaving piles from, 26
table of, *30–31*
inspections, 22–23, 26, 27, 29. *See
also* maintenance
International Log Builders'
Association, 17
Ips beetles, 30, 33

jacks and jacking, 153, *154*, 155, 156
joint tool, 72

kit homes, questions for buyers of, 12

ladders, 169
lag screws, 153, 154
landscaping, 25
lap marks, 102, *102*

latex-based caulking, 61
latex-based chinking, 59
levels, 154
Lexel (caulking), 132
lichen, 166, 168–169
LifeTime (finish colorant), 140
linseed oil, 106
LiquidWood (epoxy), 32, 39, 41, 129, 130, 134–135, 137, 140, 160
Log Builder (caulking), 62, 64, 67, 74, 75
Log Building Standards, 17
log checks, 10, 64, *64*
Log Construction Manual
(Chambers), 158
log crowns
anchoring, *148*
bevel cutting process, *142*
caulking, *149*
fitting, *148*
log restoration, 116, 142
placement of, *147*
replacement with, 142, *142, 161*
scribe fitting, 144–145, *144–145*
log ends, 18
Log Jam (chinking), 59, 67
log joints, horizontal, 65, *65*
log posts, 14
log restoration. *See also* log crowns;
log walls, bowed or shifting
in backsplash problems, 116
corner panels, board and batten, 141, *141*
full-log replacement, 153–159
half-log replacement, 150, *150, 151*
half-log siding, 162, *162*
masonry pigment, 140
for old unfinished logs, 100
painted logs, 160
patching areas, 136
patching rotted wood, 134, *134*
premilled log replacement, 156, *156*
rotted log ends, 140
strengthening log ends, 140
wood putty, *136*
wood reconstruction, 135, *135*
wooden plugs, 136
log scrapers, 136, *136*, 137
log screws, 150, 156
log spikes, 153, 154
log walls, bowed or shifting, 163, 164–165, *164, 165*